Great Potential, Many Pitfalls

China's Belt and Road Initiative (BRI), China's globe-girdling infrastructure and trade corridor project, is a rare watershed in international affairs. It affects, whether directly or indirectly, nearly the entire world, directly involving more than 60 countries, nearly 4.5 billion people (about two-thirds of the world's population), up to $8 trillion, and around 40 per cent of the global economy.

BRI also entails a rising power—perhaps the next superpower—endeavouring to build one of the biggest and most expensive super-projects the world has ever seen. If it achieves its potential, BRI could even pose a threat to the Bretton Woods global economic model that has prevailed since the end of World War II. BRI has the potential to change the world in a big way. And yet, the project also confronts security and financial challenges that are as serious as its potential is soaring. In this way, BRI is a topic that needs serious examination. This book features chapters on BRI prepared by top international scholars who have been tracking the project closely. The chapters assess the project's impact across Asia, highlight its opportunities and challenges, and consider what might be in store in the future.

The chapters in this book were first published as a special issue of the *Asian Affairs*.

Bijan Omrani is Editor of the journal *Asian Affairs*. He is author of several books, articles, and chapters on Afghanistan and Central Asia, amongst other areas. He is an honorary associate research fellow at the University of Exeter, UK.

Great Potential, Many Pitfalls

Understanding China's Belt and Road Initiative

Edited by
Bijan Omrani

Routledge
Taylor & Francis Group
LONDON AND NEW YORK

First published 2022
by Routledge
2 Park Square, Milton Park, Abingdon, Oxon, OX14 4RN

and by Routledge
605 Third Avenue, New York, NY 10158

Routledge is an imprint of the Taylor & Francis Group, an informa business

British Library Cataloguing-in-Publication Data
A catalogue record for this book is available from the British Library

ISBN13: 978-0-367-51657-4 (hbk)
ISBN13: 978-0-367-51658-1 (pbk)
ISBN13: 978-1-003-05478-8 (ebk)

Typeset in Times New Roman
by codeMantra

Publisher's Note
The publisher accepts responsibility for any inconsistencies that may have arisen during the conversion of this book from journal articles to book chapters, namely the inclusion of journal terminology.

Contents

Citation Information

The chapters in this book were originally published in the *Asian affairs*, volume 50, issue 2 (June 2019). When citing this material, please use the original page numbering for each article, as follows:

Preface
Bijan Omrani
Asian affairs, volume 50, issue 2 (June 2019) pp. 179

Introduction
Great Potential, Many Pitfalls: Understanding China's Belt and Road Initiative
Michael Kugelman
Asian affairs, volume 50, issue 2 (June 2019) pp. 180–186

Chapter 1
The Belt and Road Initiative: Modernity, Geopolitics and the Developing Global Order
Shirley Yu
Asian affairs, volume 50, issue 2 (June 2019) pp. 187–201

Chapter 2
China in Central Asia: The First Strand of the Silk Road Economic Belt
Raffaello Pantucci
Asian affairs, volume 50, issue 2 (June 2019) pp. 202–215

Chapter 3
Beijing's Response to the Belt and Road Initiative's "Pushback": A Story of Assessment and Adaptation
Nadège Rolland
Asian affairs, volume 50, issue 2 (June 2019) pp. 216–235

Chapter 4
The China–Pakistan Economic Corridor: The Lure of Easy Financing and the Perils of Poor Planning
Arif Rafiq
Asian affairs, volume 50, issue 2 (June 2019) pp. 236–248

Chapter 5
Flawed by Design: The Challenge of Flawed Democracies to China's Rise
James Schwemlein
Asian affairs, volume 50, issue 2 (June 2019) pp. 249–259

Chapter 6
Is the Belt and Road Initiative a Chinese Geo-Political Strategy?
Yiwei Wang and Xuejun Liu
Asian affairs, volume 50, issue 2 (June 2019) pp. 260–267

Chapter 7
China-Pakistan Economic Corridor – Is it the Road to the Future?
Nalanda Roy
Asian affairs, volume 50, issue 2 (June 2019) pp. 268–282

Contributors

Michael Kugelman is Asia Program Deputy Director and Senior Associate for South Asia at the Wilson Center, Washington D.C.

Xuejun Liu is Graduate student at the School of International Studies, Renmin University of China, China

Bijan Omrani is Editor of the Asian Affairs Journal.

Raffaello Pantucci is Director of International Security Studies at the Royal United Services Institute (RUSI), UK.

Arif Rafiq is non-resident fellow at the Middle East Institute in Washington, DC where he studies political reform, religious extremism, and terrorism in Pakistan, Afghanistan, and India.

Nadège Rolland is Senior Fellow for Political and Security Affairs at the National Bureau of Asian Research (NBR), a think-tank based in Seattle and Washington, Washington D.C.

Nalanda Roy is Associate Professor of International Studies and Asian Politics at Georgia Southern University. She is also the associate editor of the Journal of Asian Security and International Affairs.

James Schwemlein is nonresident scholar in the South Asia Program at the Carnegie Endowment for International Peace and a former U.S. diplomat.

Yiwei Wang holds the Jean Monnet Chair and is Director of the Institute of International Affairs and is also Director of the Center for European Studies at Renmin University of China.

Shirley Yu is fellow at the Ash Center, Harvard Kennedy School, a former China National Television News Anchor, senior executive, and board member.

PREFACE

BIJAN OMRANI

This issue of the *Asian Affairs Journal* is the second in an annual series of special issues produced as part of a collaboration between the Royal Society for Asian Affairs in London and the Woodrow Wilson International Center for Scholars in Washington DC. Last year's special issue was dedicated to the subject of religious freedom in South Asia. This year's issue is focused on the political and economic impact of the Belt and Road Initiative, particularly on the countries of South and Central Asia. It brings together many of the papers given by an international panel of experts at a joint Royal Society for Asian Affairs and Woodrow Wilson Center conference. This conference was held on 7 Jan 2019 and hosted by King's College London. A video recording of the conference can be watched online: https://www.youtube.com/watch?v=xiYpfzF-RIY (morning session); https://www.youtube.com/watch?v=q4hiwwH1kzE (afternoon session).

The Royal Society for Asian Affairs would like to take this opportunity to thank a number of individuals and institutions for making this conference and special issue possible: The Woodrow Wilson Center for Scholars, and in particular Michael Kugelman, the Center's Asia Program Deputy Director; King's College London and the Lau China Institute, and especially Professor Kerry Brown and Dr Shirley Yu; Taylor & Francis, and particularly the Area Studies Managing Director, Laurence Goodchild; and also all the participants in the January Conference.

INTRODUCTION

GREAT POTENTIAL, MANY PITFALLS: UNDERSTANDING CHINA'S BELT AND ROAD INITIATIVE

MICHAEL KUGELMAN

It's not often that something like the Belt and Road Initiative (BRI), China's globe-girdling infrastructure and trade corridor project, comes rumbling along. Indeed, BRI represents one of those rare watershed developments for international affairs – something so big and consequential that few corners of the globe, no matter how remote, can afford to ignore it. And that's because BRI affects, whether directly or indirectly, nearly the entire world.

The scale alone is extraordinary – on both statistical and strategic levels.

BRI boasts the potential to involve more than 60 countries, nearly 4.5 billion people (about two thirds of the world's population), up to $8 trillion, and around 40 per cent of the global economy. Estimates also peg it to be 12 times as large, in absolute dollar terms, as the Marshall Plan.[1] What makes the scale even more striking is that it comes on top of ample preexisting Chinese investment around the world. According to American Enterprise Institute data, the value of Beijing's total investments and contracts in Asia, Africa, and the Middle East between 2005 and 2012 – the year before BRI was officially launched – comprised billions of dollars. This financing included $10 billion in Pakistan, $14 billion in Indonesia, $20 billion in Saudi Arabia, and $15 billion in Nigeria.[2]

BRI also entails a rising power – perhaps the next superpower – endeavouring to build one of the biggest and most expensive super-projects the world has ever seen. If it achieves its potential, BRI could even pose a threat to the Bretton Woods global economic model that has prevailed since the end of World War II – one dominated by Western-led financial institutions such as the World Bank and International Monetary Fund. Indeed, BRI's emergence has been accompanied by the establishment of a key new banking institution, the Beijing-based Asian Infrastructure Investment Bank, which counts China as its top contributor.

BRI has the potential to change the world in a big way. And yet, the project also confronts security and financial challenges that are as serious as its potential is soaring. In this regard, BRI is a topic ripe for serious examination.

This issue of *Asian Affairs*, which marks the second collaboration between the Royal Society of Asian Affairs and the Washington, DC-based Woodrow Wilson Center, features essays on BRI prepared by international researchers who have been tracking the project closely. The essays assess the project's impact to this point across Asia, highlight its opportunities and challenges, and consider what might be in store in the future. These contributions were originally presented at a conference organized by the Royal Society and the Wilson Center, and hosted by King's College in London, in January 2019.

Multiple rationales, multiple routes

Beijing's official motivation for BRI is purely economic: The Chinese government wishes to facilitate greater access to far-flung markets to feed its rapidly growing economy. This entails the robust pursuit of traditional infrastructure development – such as roads, rail lines, ports, and power projects – but also newer types of infrastructure. Under the BRI rubric, Beijing intends to oversee the development of cross-border fibre-optic projects and other modern telecommunications initiatives.

Despite Beijing's stated emphasis on solely economic rationales, a likely unstated goal of BRI is to leverage investment to expand China's influence and deepen an already-entrenched global footprint. Some critics have accused Beijing of seeking this influence through malign means, including "debt trap diplomacy," whereby Chinese loans force indebted host countries to become dependent on Beijing.[3] Such allegations intensified after Sri Lanka, unable to pay loans back to Beijing, signed an entire port over to China in the form of a 99-year lease in December 2017.

Additionally, BRI has sparked suspicion among Beijing's rivals that the project may eventually include military components, such as basing facilities near BRI-financed ports. Djibouti, which hosts China's only known overseas military base, is a major recipient of Chinese infrastructure funds. A 2017 Pentagon report on China's military predicted that Beijing "likely will seek to establish additional military bases in countries with which it has longstanding, friendly relationships."[4] China has repeatedly denied rumours about a military component of BRI.

Predictably, BRI is a source of concern for the Trump Administration. The project represents one of the most concrete indications of Beijing's growing presence around the world. This deepening Chinese global footprint is concerning to Washington because the Trump administration regards Beijing as its greatest strategic rival – and as a core national security concern as well. When the Trump White House released its first national security strategy in December 2017, that document described strategic rivalry, not terrorism, as America's top national security threat.[5]

While U.S. officials haven't said so publicly, the Trump administration's Indo-Pacific strategy, announced in 2018, is likely meant to be a response to BRI, and meant to serve as a counter to China's BRI-fuelled activities. The Indo-Pacific strategy, much like the Obama administration's Asia rebalance policy, aims to increase U.S resources, both economic and military, in Asia. It also promotes the principles of free trade, open seas, and a rules-based order for the region – thereby drawing a contrast with what Washington perceives to be the predatory lending and trade-unfriendly tactics that fuel BRI's expansion. While some analysts believe U.S. officials exaggerate the negative implications of BRI – and overstate the idea of a China threat more broadly – the Trump administration is not known for espousing sanguine views about China, its policies, or its intentions.[6]

Broadly speaking, BRI intends to feature two major pathways: A continental road that links China to Europe via South and Central Asia, and a sea corridor that connects China and Europe through the Indian Ocean. These routes entail BRI-related projects in Europe, Asia, Africa, and the Middle East.

Collectively, these two pathways include five envisioned routes: The New Eurasia Land Bridge, stretching from China's Jiangsu province to the Dutch city of Rotterdam; a China-Mongolia-Russia trilateral economic corridor; a China-Central Asia-West Asia Corridor, linking China and the Arabian Peninsula; a China-Indochina Peninsula Economic

Corridor – connected by land and sea – extending from China's Pearl River Delta and Chinese rail routes into the ASEAN countries; and the China-Pakistan Economic Corridor (CPEC), connecting China's Xinjiang province to the Gwadar port in southern Pakistan. CPEC is arguably the most operationalized of these routes, with China already having completed several new BRI-financed power projects in Pakistan.

A sixth envisioned project, the Bangladesh-China-India-Myanmar Economic Corridor, will face difficulties being absorbed into the BRI rubric because India – China's regional rival – has expressed serious misgivings about BRI. New Delhi has expressed its formal opposition to CPEC, citing Chinese investment projects in Pakistan that extend into disputed territory claimed by India.

Very real risks

Supporters of BRI, including countries like Pakistan with close ties to Beijing, emphasize the project's potential advantages: Better infrastructure in poorly integrated regions; more electricity generation in energy-insecure areas; new local employment opportunities generated by upsurges in Chinese development projects; and overall the ability to bring more prosperity and stability to troubled parts of the world. It's hard to oppose results like these.

However, major obstacles threaten the emergence of these positive outcomes. One is security. BRI is envisioned to pass through some of the world's most unstable regions. While some volatile countries along the BRI route – such as Pakistan – have enjoyed security improvements in recent years, several others on or near BRI's various pathways – including Iraq, Syria, and Afghanistan – are dangerously unstable or at war. To be sure, Beijing has demonstrated a willingness to tolerate large amounts of risk in its foreign investments; in past years it has made agricultural and infrastructure investments in volatile African nations, including South Sudan and the Democratic Republic of Congo.[7] Still, China will struggle to build out BRI in areas mired in conflict or where terrorists hold sway.

Another risk is water shortage. Many areas of South Asia and the Middle East are dangerously water-insecure. Pakistan has one of the lowest rates of per capita water availability in the world. And yet it is in Pakistan where China is engaging in some of its most intensive infrastructure development – a pursuit that requires ample quantities of water. One of

BRI's signature projects – the development of the Gwadar port – is taking place in the bone-dry province of Baluchistan. Today, Gwadar's water supply is largely dependent on tankers that truck supplies in from a dam nearly 100 miles away – clearly not a sustainable solution to water insecurity.[8]

The biggest risk for BRI is financial: The very real possibility that host countries will be unable to pay loans back to Beijing. A 2018 study by the Center for Global Development (CGD), using criteria such as a country's public debt-to-GDP ratio and the concentration of that debt with China as creditor, identified 23 countries judged to be at high risk of "debt distress" from additional BRI-related financing. These nations are quite geographically dispersed, with 10 from Asia, seven from the Middle East and Africa, and six from Europe and Eurasia. Eight of these countries are singled out for being of particular concern.[9]

These eight particularly at-risk nations include Djibouti – a nation with public external debt that constitutes a whopping 85 per cent of GDP, with much of this debt owed to China Exim Bank. Another, Montenegro, has a projected debt-to-GDP ration of 83 per cent, with much of this debt emanating from a large motorway project mostly funded by Exim Bank. The list of eight is rounded out by Asian countries, including, significantly, Pakistan. CGD notes the possibility of future Pakistani public debt ratios of 70 per cent, and it flags reports that Beijing is charging Islamabad interest rates that are twice as high as those assigned to other countries.

Ominously for Beijing, several countries, fearing financial risks, have backed out of some of their BRI commitments to China. Most famously, in 2018, Malaysia's new government – riding an anti-corruption wave that helped catapult it to power – cancelled $20 billion in China-funded projects. Also, over the last year, Bangladesh and Myanmar, among others, have walked back or renegotiated earlier commitments to China, citing prohibitive costs.[10]

Whither BRI?

In sum, BRI is flush with potential, and burdened with risk. And yet, despite generating banner headlines and attracting ample attention from policymakers, there's also much that's not known about the initiative. China, being the authoritarian state that it is, does not make much information about the project publicly available. The contracts and other legal agreements governing the financing aspects of BRI are highly opaque.

The lack of information about BRI complicates efforts to forecast its fate. Will Beijing manage to work around the challenges of security and natural resource constraints? Will it renegotiate loans with host nations to make the project more financially viable? Will it push ahead in the event of sustained financial risks, or will it pull the plug on the project? These are difficult questions at this point.

With the passage of time, more clarity may emerge. After all, BRI is still a relatively young initiative. For now, however, the project should be seen for what it is: A big, flashy, once-in-a-generation phenomenon that could chart new heights and have a transformative impact on international affairs – or come crashing down to earth, a flash in the pan done in by outsize expectations and insurmountable obstacles.

ACKNOWLEDGEMENTS

The author is grateful to Wilson Center research intern Sita Kouhi for her assistance with this essay.

NOTES

1. See Jonathan Hillman, 'How Big is China's Belt and Road?'. *CSIS Commentary*, April 3, 2018, https://www.csis.org/analysis/how-big-chinas-belt-and-road and Enda Curran, 'China's Marshall Plan'. *Bloomberg*, August 7, 2016, https://www.bloomberg.com/news/articles/2016-08-07/china-s-marshall-plan (accessed 28 April 2019).
2. China Global Investment Tracker, American Enterprise Institute, http://www.aei.org/china-global-investment-tracker/ (accessed 28 April 2019).
3. John Pomfret, 'China's Debt Traps Around the World Are a Trademark of Its Imperialist Intentions'. *Washington Post*, August 27, 2018, https://www.washingtonpost.com/news/global-opinions/wp/2018/08/27/chinas-debt-traps-around-the-world-are-a-trademark-of-its-imperialist-ambitions/?utm_term=.0d474e84218c (accessed 28 April 2019).
4. 'Annual Report to Congress: Military and Security Developments Involving the People's Republic of China 2017'. *Office of the Secretary of Defense*, May 15, 2017, https://dod.defense.gov/Portals/1/Documents/pubs/2017_China_Military_Power_Report.PDF (accessed 28 April 2019).

5. National Security Strategy of the United States of America, The White House, December 2017, https://www.whitehouse.gov/wp-content/uploads/2017/12/NSS-Final-12-18-2017-0905.pdf (accessed 28 April 2019).
6. See, for example, Kishore Mahbubani, 'What China Threat? How the United States and China Can Avoid War'. *Harper's Magazine*, February 2019, https://harpers.org/archive/2019/02/what-china-threat/ (accessed 28 April 2019).
7. Gro Intelligence, 'A Look at Chinese Investment in African Agriculture'. January 23, 2015, https://gro-intelligence.com/insights/a-look-at-chinese-investment-in-african-agriculture#Background (accessed 28 April 2019).
8. Mariyam Suleman, 'Gwadar's Water Crisis'. *The Diplomat*, May 1, 2018, https://thediplomat.com/2018/05/gwadars-water-crisis/ (accessed 28 April 2019).
9. John Hurley, Scott Morris, and Gailyn Portlance, 'Examining the Debt Implications of the Belt and Road Initiative from a Policy Perspective'. *Center for Global Development, CGD Policy Paper 121*, March 2018, https://www.cgdev.org/sites/default/files/examining-debt-implications-belt-and-road-initiative-policy-perspective.pdf (accessed 28 April 2019).
10. Kari Lindberg and Tripti Lahiri, 'From Asia to Africa, China's "Debt Trap Diplomacy" Was Under Siege in 2018'. *Quartz*, December 28, 2018, https://qz.com/1497584/how-chinas-debt-trap-diplomacy-came-under-siege-in-2018/ (accessed 28 April 2019).

THE BELT AND ROAD INITIATIVE: MODERNITY, GEOPOLITICS AND THE DEVELOPING GLOBAL ORDER

SHIRLEY YU

Introduction

In March 2013, a speech was given by Chinese president Xi Jinping in Astana, Kazakhstan, initiating the strategy of the ‘Silk Road Economic Belt’. In November 2013, a further speech was given by President Xi in Jakarta, Indonesia, launching ‘the 21st Century Maritime Silk Road’. Both speeches combined marked the birth of the grand strategic vision of the fifth generation of Chinese Communist leadership. This vision is commonly referred to as the Belt and Road Initiative.

Definition of China’s Belt and Road Initiative

“The Silk Road Economic Belt” and “21st Century Maritime Silk Road” (一带一路, or “BRI” hereafter) encompasses 66 countries across Central & Eastern Eurasia and the maritime Asia Pacific. It covers 63% of the global population and over 1/3rd of the world’s GDP. It contains almost every current major world religion, and straddles six of the seven fault lines between civilizations, as envisaged by Samuel P. Huntington.

BRI is China’s unilateral vision for the future structure of the greater Eurasian region. It attempts to promote infrastructure connectivity and investment through land-locked continental Eurasia, develop efficient maritime connections from the South China Sea and Africa to Western Europe, and hopes to exert China’s comprehensive geo-economic, geopolitical and strategic influence in the whole region.

Figure 1 Map of the BRI

In 2015, a book entitled *One Belt One Road, China's Top National Strategy* was published with an official endorsement, signalling that the BRI had become China's overriding National Strategy. I equate China's BRI to the Grand Strategy of the U.S. post-WWII in its international significance and objectives. The U.S. over this period of time established multilateral financial institutions including the IMF and the World Bank, and supranational institutions including the United Nations. It initiated the Marshall Plan to promote regional economic growth, NATO as the regional security framework, and the Bretton Woods

Table 1 BRI's Regional institutions in comparison to the current global mechanisms

Multilateral institutional mechanism	BRI region	Global order
Regional Trade Integration	16 + 1 Regional Comprehensive Economic partnership ASEAN + 3 BRI Economic Corridor	WTO European Union
Regional Financial Integration	Asian Infrastructure Investment Bank Silk Road Fund New Development Bank	The World Bank
Regional Military Security Organization	Shanghai Cooperation Organization	NATO
Lender of Last Resort and Supranational Organization	To be developed	IMF United Nations

system to establish the U.S. Dollar-standard for the global monetary system. China has built a comparable multilateral regional framework over this period, very similar to the grand strategy of the U.S. post-WWII.

There has been much speculation about the total scale of investment under China's BRI. Popular estimates range from $1 trillion to $8 trillion[1] across the established multilateral investment platforms and debt financing through China's policy banks, including the China Development Bank and EXIM Bank.

China's BRI works in coordination with President Xi's Two 'One Hundred Year Plans'. The first One Hundred Year Plan is that by 2021, upon the centennial anniversary of the founding of the Chinese Communist Party, China should reach the living standards of the poorer countries in Europe. The other is that by 2049, China should attain 'modernity', and be among the greatest nations of the world. The Belt and Road Initiative will serve as China's transitory grand strategy between 2013 and around 2050. If BRI were executed successfully over the coming three decades, China's ultimate grand strategy by 2050 would be to assert a Chinese version of a global order. Just as the Post-WWII grand strategy of the U.S. served as the means for the ultimate foreign policy objective of Pax-Americana, BRI is China's grand strategy, but not the end in itself of China's grand strategy, rather a means to its ultimate end, i.e. Pax-Sinica.

Deconstruction of China's BRI

1) *The BRI is about economics, but not simply about economics.*

President Xi Jinping's BRI was postulated as a two-pronged vision. One is the Modernization Vision, and the other, the Common Destiny Vision. The first one is clearly economic, and the latter, political.

The Modernization Vision, in Xi's own words, is for regional countries to 'jump onto China's economic high-speed rail'. To paraphrase the jargon, BRI countries will participate in China's economic prosperity through infrastructure development and infrastructure investments made possible by China.

The Common Destiny Vision, in President Xi's own articulations, is for regional countries to build a 'Community of Common Destiny'.[2] During his speech in Davos in 2017, Xi's regional vision further transcended to a grander 'Common Destiny as Humankind'.[3] This vision captivates a high moral ideal and invites much more complex dialogues than simple understanding of the BRI as a common economic policy prescription for the region. A 'community of common destiny' elevates the BRI to similar strategic significance as the Manifest Destiny, a founding principle of U.S. foreign policy. The declaration of China's vision of a global destiny has essentially promulgated China's quest for its own version of a world order.

> 2) *The success of the BRI is contingent upon the cohesion and integrity of the achievement of both visions in its entirety.*

The modernization vision

Infrastructure investments and the long-term accessibility to financing which China provides will have a positive effect on the BRI countries' economic growth, and therefore enhance the living standards of BRI countries. This is largely in accordance with developmental economics. It should be stressed that development is taking place both in heavy infrastructure, such as railways and highways, and also digital communications and the internet. It has become clear that dollar-for-dollar, investments in modern communications technology have a far greater return than from money invested in traditional infrastructure developments, such as railways and highways. The telecom infrastructure networks led by Huawei and ZTE are currently expanding rapidly through the BRI region. Further, China's success in setting and leading the global telecommunications standards particularly in 5G will be more fundamental in shaping economic development patterns of the region than the expansion of physical infrastructures over a wide geographical scale.

The common destiny vision

What are the geopolitical implications for the region with the modernization of the countries along the BRI? The answer to this question is essentially a revival of the decades-long debate that started with political scientist Seymour Lipset. Lipset tested the causal relationship between a country's economic development and its political openness.[4] He further advanced the conclusion that democracy is the outcome of economic development. This 'Modernization–Democratization' concept has since been tested, retested, and contested, and generated a large number of political analyses in the field over the past few decades. It is significant in understanding the future direction of the BRI region as regional countries go through economic modernization supported by China.

If Lispet, his followers including former President Bill Clinton, and the believers in the Washington Consensus were right, BRI countries would have a tendency to become democracies as they economically develop. These countries would then naturally be inclined to align themselves with countries of the West, believe in Western values and, for all practical purposes become part of the West. Therefore, despite the development of the BRI, there would be no common destiny between China and the 65 regional BRI countries as they carried on their course of economic development. Further, democracy would be revealed as the common destiny of these economically developed nations. This is certainly not the desired outcome of Xi's vision. However, empirical analysis drawn on economic data from the World Bank and political data from the EIU Global Democracy Ranking suggests that as the BRI regional countries develop economically, there is no significant tendency for them to turn towards liberal democracy, and that Lipset's hypothesis does not reflect the practical reality in these circumstances.[5] This may be disappointing to the liberal West. However, this tendency makes Xi's Common Destiny vision possible. Therefore, the achievement of both the Chinese economic and political visions of the BRI becomes feasible.

3) *The success of the BRI is predicated upon the continued success of the China Model and the political preferences of the countries in the region.*

According to the Economist Intelligence Unit's global democracy rankings 2015, of the 66 countries in the BRI region, two countries are full democracies, i.e. the Czech Republic and New Zealand. There 24 'flawed democracies', including countries in Southern Europe and in South Asia. There are 17 hybrid regimes, including Singapore, Turkey, and various ASEAN countries, and Iraq; and 23 authoritarian regimes, including the Gulf countries, Central Asian countries, and countries in North Africa.

The China Model is essentially built upon political authoritarianism and a certain degree of economic liberalization, selected privatization and limited industry deregulation, often classified as authoritarian capitalism. Due to the natural political profile of the BRI region being predominantly quasi-democracies, failed democracies and autocracies, the China Model would allow these countries to develop economically, while still maintaining tight political control by the people in power. When faced with a dire need for economic development, regional countries are offered a choice between the China Model, and the Washington Consensus model. With their governments having little desire to forego their authoritarian powers, many of these countries would opt to choose China as a viable partner, sometimes even a preferred partner, in their development process. The diverse backgrounds of authoritarian regimes and the lack of full liberal democracy in the BRI region essentially provides China with the political incubator to expand its model of authoritarian capitalism. Therefore, the success and sustainability of the economic strategy of the BRI is essentially a competition over economic effectiveness and efficiency delivered between market authoritarianism and market liberalism, or the competition between the China Model and the Washington Consensus model. The success and sustainability are externally predicated upon the choices made by countries in the region based on their unique political economic preferences.

The political philosophical foundations of Xi's BRI 'Common destiny'

There is a clear set of common destinies that belong to the West, including liberal democracy, market liberalism and civil liberties. The Chinese-posited Common Destiny, by contrast, can only be drawn from a rich repository of Chinese history and its successive civilizations.

Absolute sovereignty and authoritarianism mandated by Confucius

Post-Westphalia, the concept of modern sovereignty was born.[6] However, the power of sovereigns was never absolute in Europe.[7] A king's sovereign power in Europe was bound either by the power of the aristocracy, or by the power of divinity. Sovereigns were dependent on the aristocrats for their military forces, and often times, for their very existence.

Chinese feudal history started earlier and lasted longer than European nation-states. The power of the sovereigns in China was never bound by the power of the aristocracy. In 211 BC, Qin Shi Huang, the first emperor of China, invented a civil service selection system run on meritocracy that remained virtually unchanged throughout Chinese history. In many ways, it is still used today.[8] The civil service apparatus was organized hierarchically, which ended with the emperor himself. The complex selection system was exercised through a national exam, and civil servants were selected based on merit. Because the mandarin positions were not inheritable, the emperors were left with absolute power with no prospect of sabotage from his aristocrats.

In the West, the role of religion was another major hedge on the absolute power of the sovereigns. The Holy Roman Empire and the Catholic Church both sought to unite nation-states in Europe under a single authority, a form of Imperium Christianum. This culminated in the Thirty Years' War which resulted in the concession of power by both the Empire and the Church to the power of the Sovereigns.

Chinese sovereignty on the other hand, was never bound by the power of religion. The most dominant religions, Buddhism and Confucianism,[9] did not provide a means to check the exercise of political authority. Buddhism originated from a set of psychological and ontological assumptions totally unlike those of modern Western thought. In contrast to Christianity, Buddhism defines the enlightenment of the individual by the very denial of his ontological existence. A consequence of Buddhist belief is that the very rights that are intrinsically attached to the very existence of an individual from the Western viewpoint – individual liberty and civil rights, core beliefs of Western liberalism – are not acknowledged as being valid.

Confucianism supported a moral code of civil obedience, from the inferior to the superior, and all the way to the Emperor, the 'Son of Heaven'. This created a hierarchical system that paid respects and tributes to the elder, the superior and the higher authority. Confucianism does not challenge the supreme power of the sovereign. The power of the sovereign was bound by no religion, but by the Mandate of Heaven, or indeed, from another and perhaps truer viewpoint of the same idea, by his own moral limitations. In other words, even though Confucius did not endorse despotism, Confucianism did endorse authoritarianism.[10]

The Confucian view of world order: 'All Under Heaven' constructed on political heterogeneity

The Community of Common Destiny is an attempt by China to reestablish in the modern age a Chinese version of a global order. The first vision China offered was 'All Under Heaven' (天下), which dated back to at least the Qin Dynasty (second century BC), if not earlier. 'All Under Heaven' was a state-based tributary system of organizing the world order. It was run on two core beliefs. One belief was that China was the cultural centre of the world. The second belief was a consequence of the first, that all foreign rulers were expected to recognize the prominence and superiority of China.[11]

Contrary to the Western practice of colonialism, by which colonial powers conquered and ruled the inferior nations by hard power, the tributary system of imperial China was about recognizing China's superior cultural power, and thus that China ruled the tributary states by its soft power. In the 1420s, when Chinese navigator Zheng Ho sailed along what is today the Maritime Silk Road, he simply demanded that locals should kowtow to the scrolls of the Son of Heaven [the Chinese Emperor], and brought back exotic animals as tributes to the Ming court. Otherwise, these countries were left intact.

Other than the system of 'All under Heaven', Confucianism also defines the relationship between harmony and uniformity. In the Analects, it is stated, 'noble men aim at harmony, but not at uniformity. Little men aim at uniformity, but not at harmony'.[12] (君子和而不同, 小人同而不和). A Chinese approach places a priority on harmony over uniformity. China's modern foreign policy affirms that China is adaptable in working with autocracies, theocracies, democracies and authoritarian states without placing ideological biases. 'All Under Heaven' is the belief that every nation state, as an independent actor, can come under China's economic and cultural sphere without having to become homogenous on political and ideological grounds.

Western liberalism posits the exact moral contrary. The value priority is placed on uniformity, not harmony. The concept of Democratic Peace, which can be traced back to Kant, states that democracies are not likely to go to war with other democracies. It is the ideological uniformity that is essential to peace. Countries that are not in uniformity cannot be trusted, and therefore are more likely to go to war with each other. U.S. Wilsonianism, a dominant school of Twentieth Century international relations, is a reflection of the global effort to create uniformity across nations, based on the image of the U.S.

China's market authoritarianism

The 'Beijing Consensus', a term coined by Joshua Cooper Ramo, was framed as a theoretical and pragmatic economic and social model based on the speed and scale of China's economic growth, and China's political unpredictability.[13] Despite this coinage, there is by no means a clearly articulated set of economic policies from Beijing as an antithesis to the 'Washington Consensus'.[14] In a way, the truth behind the 'Beijing Consensus' is that there has been no Beijing consensus.

However, China has beyond doubt embraced an alternative path of economic development from the economic commandments of the 'Washington Consensus'. With it, China adopts a very different social and political superstructure that ensures the efficiency and stability of its economic model thus far. This in totality presents a formidable 'China Model'.

There has been certainly a resurgence in the weight and role of State-Owned Enterprises (SOEs) in the Chinese economy during Xi's reign. Mergers of major state-owned companies to create colossal Chinese enterprises in key economic sectors have occurred more frequently, making it extremely difficult for private companies to compete in key economic sectors with the SOEs. BRI projects, mostly situated in emerging economies, are inherently imbedded with varying degrees of political and economic risks. State-Owned enterprises, with a large amount of financial backing from the state, and their majority ownership being the state (unlike private enterprises), can represent Chinese state strategic interests in many ways, and secure a much bigger share of BRI investments than their private company counterparts.

Should the China Model be seen as economically successful, and at the same time non-ideological and non-interventionist, many countries along the BRI region, especially the quasi-democracies and autocracies, would welcome it as an alternative, maybe as a preferred alternative to satisfy their desire for economic growth without compromising on political authority.[15] Thus regional countries with a dire need for economic growth will be left to choose one of two alternatives: market liberalism or market authoritarianism models.

In conclusion, under the Chinese 'Common Destiny' vision, the region will likely tend towards national sovereignty over individual liberty, market authoritarianism over market liberalism, political authoritarianism over democracy, and civil obedience over civil liberty. Just as democracy, market liberalism and civil liberty define the common destiny of the West, the common destiny China envisions can be defined as nationalism, market authoritarianism and rule by civil obedience.

Implications for the transforming global order

1) *The Return of Mackinder's Eurasian Heartland Pivot*

The BRI encompasses two principal groups of routes: the continental routes and the maritime routes.

The game changer is most likely to happen in continental Eurasia. The U.S. has not been a major Eurasian continental power, especially in the Eurasian heartland, either during the Cold War or post the Cold War, either economically or ideologically. The U.S. had a military stronghold in Afghanistan during the War in Afghanistan. Since the military pullback from Afganistan, the U.S. has volunteered to forsake its strategic position in the Eurasian heartland. Meanwhile, China's infrastructure investment initiative will create new continental economic efficiencies, open borders and intra-regional trade. Given all considerations, China's economic integration efforts in the region could potentially recalibrate the balance of power on the Eurasian continent.

In the Maritime Asia-Pacific region, the power status quo will remain intact for the foreseeable future. China will largely embrace a more defensive posture. All the island disputes will remain a security issue and will get resolved one way or another, at least in the view of Henry Kissinger.[16] The U.S. has indisputable military superiority in maritime Asia, and China stays a second, but a rising second. China should understand fully that even with a potential challenge to U.S. hegemony, it is not likely to bring about a change to U.S. hegemony.

The rivalry over the Eurasian Heartland marks a historical return of Mackinder's Heartland theory from his celebrated article on the 'Geographical Pivot of History'.[17] In 1904, Sir Halford Mackinder famously argued that much of the Eurasian heartland, today large parts of Russia and Central Asia, was the key to global balance of power. In Mackinder's conception,[18] whoever rules East Europe commands the Heartland; whoever rules the Heartland commands the World-Island; and whoever rules the World-Island commands the world.

The Eurasian heartland remains the world's geopolitical pivot, an idea as true a hundred years ago as it is today. The Eurasian heartland is the BRI's birthplace, a necessary corridor for the Chinese-envisioned new continental economic reality, and the foundation of a Chinese-initiated regional security pact, the Shanghai Cooperation Organization.

2) *The Asian version of the Monroe Doctrine*

In 2014, Chinese president Xi claimed that 'Asian affairs should be handled by Asians',[19] essentially an Asian version of the 'Monroe Doctrine'. There were two main implications to this statement. First, the Monroe Doctrine was defensive in nature. Although the rhetoric of the

Asian version may sound provocative, the intention is likewise not aggressive. Two, with the Monroe Doctrine, the U.S. claimed its de facto leadership of the Americas. China sees itself in similar capacity in Asia Pacific with its proclamation of the Asian Version as well.

3) *Structural transfer of power between the maritime and continental forces of world's geography*

Mackinder also famously defined the two forces of world's geography: the continental 'inner crescent' of Europe, the Middle East, South and East Asia; and the oceanic 'outer crescent' of the Americas, Britain, South Africa, Australasia and Japan.[20] Over the immediate past six centuries, the outer crescent has risen to dominate the world. Prior to the emergence of naval powers, the inner crescent had dominated the world's power-play for over two millennia or longer.

Human ingenuity precipitates the natural courses of history.[21] Naval strength has enabled faster and wider global trade through sea than on land, which gave rise to the outer crescent powers. Today, China's railway and telecommunications infrastructure development expertise is fast progressing to a level of efficiency that can fundamentally transfer global power gravity from sea back to land.

The BRI is circumstantial in a sense that China happens to be the largest economy in greater Eurasia at this particular juncture in history. But there is also something more structural, and more historically natural about it, which is the transfer of the world's power gravity between land and sea, or between the inner crescent and the outer crescent.

This competition over the Eurasian heartland is fundamentally a structural transfer of power between the political forces of the land-based authoritarian states and those of the sea-based democratic states. At the heart of this geopolitical rivalry, there lies the geo-economic competition over the efficiency of global trade and investment via land and sea routes. When the economic and trade realities change, so changes the world's geopolitical reality.

4) *A spherical view of future global order*

We often in policy discourse refer to a U.S.-led global order and China's quest for a China-centric global order. The implications to the future global order go deeper than semantics. The Western understanding of global order is one in linearity, with the global hegemon leading from the top. The second largest power in the linear order is inherently a threat to the hegemon. This 'Thucydides Trap'[22] thus becomes a highly probable event as the aspiring challenger continues to rise. All other major powers in this order are also lined up in a linear hierarchy. They inherently compete with one another, but also cooperate to uphold the integrity of the systems and the original political philosophical foundations of which this linear world order is composed. In this linear global order, the underlying intrinsic values of the nation states remain homogenous across all member nations. Competition defines the relative positions of the nation states, but does not pose a challenge to the homogeneity of the common pursuit of the West.

The Chinese-posited notion of a community of Common destiny, if it were to come to pass, would be a revival of the ancient notion of 'All Under Heaven'. It is a spherical global order with China at its centre. Contrary to the Western order in linearity, the Chinese view of a global order involves a centre and peripheral nations in a spherical formation. In this spherical global order, political and value homogeneity are not required. Unlike in the linear order where every nation has the potential to become the next hegemon, in the spherical order, it takes one nation to become the centre and no other nation is believed to have the characteristics and quality to replace the centre and to behave in the same capacity. There is not a second centre in the spherical global order, nor is there a challenger to the centre; therefore the preconditions for a Thucydides Trap do not exist in this order. The role of the centre nation is not to lead, but to stabilize the order. The centre does not strive to form allies and friends, and contain aliens and foes among the peripheral nations. All peripheral nations are viewed with no ideological bias. The centre stays as a lonely power demanding its superior nation-state status and respect by all the peripheral nations. This spherical global order reduces power competitions made in pursuit of hegemony imbedded in the linear global order. It builds a whole new understanding of the structure and mechanisms of a global institutional framework that is based on political heterogeneity. In the coming three decades, the linear global order led by the US and the spherical global order posited by China will need to find a way to sit alongside each other as the future global order morphs into its new form.

5) *The BRI is China's all-in geopolitical means towards its end pursuit of a Pax-Sinica*

Countries tend to follow more hefty ideals than hard power dominance. The Pax-Americana is a living example of global peace and order ensured through a combination of hard power and soft power of the hegemon. As discussed, one fundamental premise of the ancient 'All Under Heaven' was the recognition of China's cultural superiority, or China's soft power. It equally applies in the modern Chinese concept of global order. China has not yet formulated the soft power in the field of ideas, a set of values that is inspiring enough for the rest of the world to follow. Before China defines its ideas through which it hopes to yield its soft power, China will continue to use its hard economic power to expand its regional economic and geopolitical influence, and establish practical global institutional frameworks to propel its multilateral agenda. The prevalence of political and economic illiberalism in the region provides the perfect incubator for the spread of China's unique political economic model and success of its geopolitical quest. The BRI will be China's all-in means to achieve its ultimate foreign policy end, the establishment of a Chinese version of global order based on a combination of China's hard economic and military powers and soft power of the ideas through to the midpoint of the 21st Century.

Over the coming decades, from a political philosophical perspective, the world will continue to see a clash between the Jeffersonian egalitarian liberalism, and competitive visions of global common destinies between 'beacon on the hill' and 'all under heaven'.

Conclusion

We are likely to see a paradigm shift in the world order in the coming decades, centred around The BRI as China's signature foreign policy.

The BRI aims to achieve both an economic vision and a political vision. With China providing infrastructure investment and infrastructure development expertise to regional countries, it would help regional countries develop economically, or to share China's economic prosperity. As these countries develop economically, on account of the unique political profile of the region being predominantly failed democracies, quasi-democracies and autocracies, these countries will not exhibit a significant tendency to lean towards full liberal democracy. The fact that they won't fall into the Western camp as they economically develop provides China with an opportunity to realize its second BRI vision, to form a community of common destiny with the regional countries. The common destiny China posits would be drawn from a fusion of Chinese ancient philosophy and its modern political ideology. It would be composed of elements including authoritarianism, nationalism and rule by civil obedience. The success and survivability of the BRI is contingent upon China's continued ability to succeed with its China Model, its ability to protect is massive amount of asset ownership overseas and the unique political preferences of countries in the region.

Stephen Halper said, 'China's greatest fear is American ideas'.[23] It is equally true that America's greatest fear should be China's ideas. Before China masters the power of its own ideas, China's economic interest in the region will inevitably be protected and secured by its rising military strength. China is left with virtually no other means to ensure its regional economic interests beyond its borders, other than the ready use of security means, as the recipients of China's infrastructure investments include many illiberal and unpredictable regimes, which lack transparency and legal safeguards.

The BRI in the coming decades will be China's most significant foreign policy objective in the most strategic region in establishing its global power, due to both the region's geographical proximity to China and regional countries' political economic preferences. It is crucial for the West to engage with this grand strategic concept of China's version of a global destiny through a deliberate set of policy choices including selective engagement, selective rejection, selective competition and selective accommodation.

NOTES

1. Jonathan Hillman, Center for Strategic & International Studies. https://www.csis.org/analysis/how-big-chinas-belt-and-road (accessed 28 April 2019).
2. Jinping Xi, Boao Forum for Asia, May, 2015. http://news.xinhuanet.com/politics/2015-03/28/c_1114794507.htm (accessed 28 April 2019).
3. Jinping Xi, Davos World Economic Forum, 2017. http://wap.chinadaily.com.cn/2017-01/17/content_27982053.htm (accessed 28 April 2019).
4. Seymour Martin Lipset, 'Some Social Requisites of Democracy: Economic Development and Political Legitimacy'. *American Political Science Review* Vol. 53. Issue 1 (1959): 69–105.
5. GDP per capita, World Bank Databank, 2015; Democracy Ranking, EIU, 2015.
6. Hendrik Spruyt, *The Sovereign State and Its Competitors: An Analysis of Systems Change*. Princeton Studies in International History and Politics. Princeton, NJ: Princeton University Press, 1994, pp. 153–181.
7. Andrew Coleman and Jackson Nyamuya Maogoto, '"Westphalian" Meets "Eastphalian" Sovereignty: China in a Globalized World'. *Asian Journal of International Law* Vol. 3. Issue 2 (2013): 246.

8. Ibid., pp. 237–269.
9. Confucianism here can be considered as a way of ethical religious teaching.
10. Coleman and Maogoto, '"Westphalian" Meets "Eastphalian" Sovereignty', op. cit., pp. 237–269.
11. Ranbir Vohra, *China's Path to Modernization: A Historical Review from 1800 to the Present*, 2nd ed. Englewood Cliffs, NJ: Prentice Hall, 1992.
12. *The Analects of Confucius: An Online Teaching Translation*, 2015 (Version 2.2), Robert Eno, Book 13.23. http://www.indiana.edu/~p374/Analects_of_Confucius_(Eno-2015).pdf (accessed 28 April 2019).
13. Joshua Cooper Ramo, 'The Beijing Consensus', Foreign Policy Center/Publication, May 2004.
14. John Williamson, 'What Washington Means by Policy Reform', in John Williamson (Ed.), *Latin American Adjustment: How Much Has Happened?* Washington: Peterson Institute for International Economics, 1990.
15. Bridget Welsh, and Alex Chang, 'Choosing China: Public Perceptions of "China as a Model"'. *Journal of Contemporary China* Vol. 24. Issue 93 (2015): 1–15.
16. Henry Kissinger, Dialogue with Graham Allison, Harvard Club of New York, 2017.
17. Halford John MacKinder, 'Geographical Pivot of History'. *The Geographical Journal*, Vol. 23. Issue 4 (April 1904): 421–437.
18. Halford John Mackinder, *Democratic Ideals and Reality: A Study in the Politics of Reconstruction*. New York: Henry Holt, 1919, pp. 79–84.
19. Jinping Xi, Speech at 4th Conference on Interaction and Confidence-Building Measures in Asia Summit. http://www.chinanews.com/gn/2014/05-21/6195322.shtml (accessed 28 April 2019).
20. Halford MacKinder, 'Geographical Pivot of History'. *Polis: Politicheskie Issledovaniya* Vol. 5. Issue 4 (1995): 162.
21. Nick Megoran and Sevara Sharapova, *Central Asia in International Relations*, Introduction, p. 9.
22. The notion that a clash between the rising power and the hegemon is inevitable, based on the clash of Athens and Sparta in the fifth century BC.
23. Stefan Halper, *The Beijing Consensus: How China's Authoritarian Model Will Dominate the Twenty-first Century*. New York: Basic Books, 2010, p. 208.

CHINA IN CENTRAL ASIA: THE FIRST STRAND OF THE SILK ROAD ECONOMIC BELT

RAFFAELLO PANTUCCI

To understand the Belt and Road Initiative, Central Asia is a good place to start. The broader vision that has been laid out as the Belt and Road was born out of a pair of speeches delivered in Kazakhstan and Indonesia in 2013.[1] The decision to start with Astana, Kazakhstan was not an accident. Laying out his concept for a Silk Road Economic Belt that would tie China across the Eurasian heartland to Europe, Xi Jinping was in essence stamping his branding on something that had been taking place for almost two decades previously as Beijing's westernmost province of Xinjiang sought development and did this through growing economic integration into its immediate economic neighbourhood. In many ways, the Belt and Road Initiative is the internationalization of a policy that had been playing out in Central Asia for many years prior, turning this regional approach into a brand that became the articulation for Chinese foreign policy under Xi Jinping. Therefore, to understand how the Belt and Road might play out in the future, it is useful to look back to Central Asia.

China's history with Central Asia is as young as the countries themselves. Born out of the end of the Cold War and a need to determine China's borders with the former Soviet space, the "Shanghai Five" grouping was initially a format to bring together the five leaders of China, Kazakhstan, Kyrgyzstan, Russia, and Tajikistan to seek to delineate their borders. Having created this format and achieved some success in determining their borders and other security issues amongst themselves, in 2001, the grouping was expanded to include Uzbekistan and formalized into a multilateral organization called the Shanghai Cooperation Organization (SCO). Two Secretariats were established – one in Beijing, and one in Tashkent to focus on counter-terrorism as the Regional Anti-Terrorism

Structure (RATS). Every member of the organization joined the SCO for different reasons, with the newly independent countries of Central Asia keen to join any multilateral organization where they were given an equal voice. For Russia, the aim was to keep a check on Chinese activity in their backyard, while for China it was an attempt to create a vehicle that would help with their economic engagement with their immediate neighbourhood in Central Asia.[2]

But this aspect of Chinese engagement under the SCO never really came to pass. Any Chinese attempt to create economic structures under the organization were frustrated by the other members who resisted China's attempts to push the organization in an economic direction. Chinese experts and officials would regularly advance presentations replete with ideas for what an SCO Free Trade Area would look like[3], how the SCO could create a development bank[4], and what joint accounts China could help foster under the organization. During a visit to Central Asia in 2012 the author heard about construction projects after the riots in Kyrgyzstan being planned under the auspices of the SCO.[5] And Central Asian members would occasionally raise the prospect of hosting institutions under the bigger organization.[6] However, these were largely blocked (with some exceptions, like a coordinating Interbank body which sought to bring together regional development banks to coordinate projects and investment[7] – though it is unclear the degree to which this has actually happened) and instead the organization moved in an increasingly security direction as the members concluded that the issues they most easily agreed on were associated with hard power security questions.[8] Counter-terrorism in particular became a banner around which all of the members could gather. For all the powers, the fear of anti-state groups (whom they defined as terrorists) mobilizing against the government was a major concern, and therefore provided a useful convening concept around which they could all agree.

For China, the long-term answer to these difficult security questions is economic prosperity. The creation of a context in which people are able to become rich is a context from which stability would flow. Prosperity would mean that they would reject terrorist ideas (defined in China as separatism, extremism and terrorism – a founding concept at the core of the SCO). Consequently, the push to improve prosperity in the Chinese concept became a key to dealing with the fundamental security issue which Beijing's leadership worried about.

The problem for Beijing is that Xinjiang is a region as far from China's prosperous coasts as the landlocked Central Asian countries to which it is adjacent. Consequently, in order to develop Xinjiang, Beijing needs to upgrade the economic fortunes of the region adjacent to Xinjiang in Central Asia. For Xinjiang to become as prosperous as China's eastern seaboard cities and regions, it would need to be more open economically to its immediate regions and more able to benefit from trade with and through them across the Eurasian heartland. This vision was one that was not new to Xi Jinping, but was rather a logic that had been regularly advanced by Chinese leaders as the answer to the lack of prosperity in China's heartland.

It was not clear, however, whether this vision was delivering success nor that much effort had been dedicated towards it. For China's leadership, the priority was China's richer coastal cities and Xinjiang was largely left to the governorship of regional leaders. While Xinjiang was strategically important and occupied a space which was adjacent to some potentially problematic countries, Beijing's leadership attention was focused elsewhere, primarily the United States and national domestic economic growth. Xinjiang, it was largely hoped, would eventually be dragged along with the rest of the country.

But things were rudely brought to a head in July 2009 in the wake of horrendous riots in Xinjiang which led to the deaths of over 200 citizens and the apparent loss of control in one of China's provincial capitals, Urumqi. The situation was such that then-leader Hu Jintao was obligated to leave an international G8 gathering in L'Aquila, Italy to rush home to manage the situation.[9] In the wake of these terrible events, it was clear that a revisiting of China's approach to Xinjiang was needed whereby the previous approach of largely leaving the story to play out according to a timetable set by the regional governor Wang Lequan was no longer working.

Rather, in the wake of the riots, a series of steps were taken. Senior figures in the region, including Wang Lequan, were moved on, and a major work conference was convened on the region. Amongst the many outcomes was a renewed push to develop the region's economy, focusing on linking its poorer sections with China's richer coastal cities. Ideas, party cadres, funding and more were linked to the specific parts of Xinjiang, alongside a massive re-allocation of capital and effort within China to help push the region to prosper. The result was to also increase the volume of support and effort going across China's borders into Central

Asia as well. For these economic opportunities to work in Xinjiang they would need markets to access and places to export their goods to. As Wen Jiabao put it to the Second China Eurasian Expo, the goal was to make Urumqi, Xinjiang's capital, "the gateway to Eurasia".[10]

This meant more construction and development was needed, in terms of opening up markets, helping develop local economies and improving connectivity. This was the logic that had largely been advanced earlier, but failed to deliver. It was a vision that was now delivered through financing provided by state owned policy banks who would offer loans to Central Asian countries to hire Chinese firms to implement projects in their countries.[11] This was matched with a feverish building spree within China, with Xinjiang's many links with Central Asia re-built and strengthened. Roads, rail, dry ports, crossing points were all needed to help improve Xinjiang's ability to trade and improve its economy. Starting in Xinjiang, going through Central Asia and ultimately to reach over to the other end of the Eurasian continent, the aim was to use connectivity to transform and develop Xinjiang and its immediate region.[12]

First formally advanced in the wake of the 2009 riots, the idea was one that became with time the foundational concept which became the Belt and Road Initiative. Coming into power in 2012, President Xi saw what was taking place in Xinjiang and, bolstered by academic ideas advanced by Peking University's then-dean of the School of International Studies, Wang Jisi, decided that the underlying approach being undertaken in Central Asia was one that was more broadly applicable.[13] Rather than let the connectivity story be one that played out only through natural economic geography, President Xi decided to inculcate the concept as China's main foreign policy concept.[14]

The narrative offered is in many ways a deeply attractive one. From Beijing's perspective, the central thrust of foreign policy was to develop trade and economic corridors emanating out from China. Making money and improving prosperity becomes the articulation of China's foreign policy with the world. This becomes the central articulation of the Belt and Road as delivered through speeches in Astana, Kazakhstan and Jakarta, Indonesia – the first being a very conscious choice to highlight the connection to China's earlier policies towards Central Asia.[15]

From an analyst's perspective, this therefore provides a useful case study for China's broader vision. If Central Asia is the first strand of the Belt and Road, and it is a corridor which has been going in some gradual form or another since the end of the Cold War with a supercharging in 2010, it provides a useful model to understand the broader consequences of China's approaches under the Belt and Road.

To understand what this looks like in practice, it is useful to focus on three aspects of China's relations with Central Asia in turn: economics, politics and security, and to assume a longer analytical view in considering what the impact has been of China's developing relations in Central Asia in particular. While from Beijing's perspective, these three are deeply intertwined with economics as the single-minded focus, the reality is that it is almost impossible to detach them from each other. The relationship between a state's economic welfare, its political life and security posture is almost impossible to completely separate – a reality which somewhat complicates the non-interference concept that lies at the heart of Beijing's view of its relationship with the world.

The economics of China and Central Asia flows through three main axes: extractives, infrastructure and markets. And in every case, the relationship is one which is far more complicated and substantial than is often captured through easy characterizations. For example, while China is increasingly one of Central Asia's largest consumers of hydrocarbons, it is also a major purchaser (and owner) of copper, zinc and gold mines. In addition, Chinese agribusiness has an ever-expanding footprint in the region, and growing deals have been established to bring agricultural products from Central Asia to Chinese markets.[16]

A growing volume of this material is moved along on roads that are built by Chinese contractors, as well as through rail links that have been increasingly refurbished and built by them across the region connecting through expanded land ports in Khorgos and the Dzungarian Pass.[17] But Chinese infrastructure stretches far beyond just building roads and rail – Chinese firms are delivering telecoms infrastructure, energy infrastructure (power stations, power lines, and home metering systems), as well as a wide range of other construction opportunities. For example, Chinese cement firms have focused on expanding their presence in the region both to help physically build infrastructure while also expanding their markets.[18]

All of this economic activity has a natural overspill into local politics, in terms of local leaders seeking Chinese support as well as China recognizing that it needs to ensure that it has won over local populations to its projects. From Beijing's perspective, this is delivered through a web of influence activities that are both covert and obvious, while at the same time to some degree a natural reflection of the changing economic geography that is taking place across the region. For example, China has established Confucius Institutes at a number of institutions across the region as well as provided Hanban teachers to language Universities in Turkmenistan. Chinese Ambassadors are increasingly present in the local press, and participants in local discourse.[19]

But in some ways most striking is the growing presence of young Central Asians who are studying or have some experience in China. This is either as students seeking opportunities in China, being pushed by their parents to study Chinese to enable easier market trading opportunities for family businesses, or more simply taking advantage of the volume of scholarships that China offers to young or mid-career Central Asians. Visit most Ministries and a growing volume of people can be found who have some functional Mandarin; visit major Chinese cities like Shanghai, Urumqi or Beijing and growing numbers of Central Asian students can be found.[20] All of this suggests a generation which is growing up with an orientation and view of the world which is more shaped by relations with China than the West. While the West remains an aspirational target for most young people, and the region still appeals to its European heritage, China's long-term soft influence is palpably growing.

This soft power stretches into the security arena where China has increased its footprint in the region through support for local security forces and the provision of training and equipment, as well as a growing volume of didactic programmes that are growing the percentage of officers who speak workable Mandarin or have spent some time in China. This is most visible through the creation of the China National Institute for SCO International Exchange and Judicial Cooperation (CNISCO), which was established at the Shanghai University of Politics and Law to provide a place where interior and border security forces from across SCO countries could come and train.[21] Previous programmes were more basic and simply focused on bringing individuals or teams to Nanjing to study Mandarin, and into Xinjiang to train alongside local security forces. This all comes atop long-established programmes bringing Central Asian security officials to China's premier security training institutions like the Academy of Military Sciences or National Defence University.[22]

Focusing in particular on Central Asia, China has also undertaken a growing volume of bilateral training exercises through the SCO. A large number of the broader SCO "Peace Mission" joint exercises seem focused on training with Russia, providing the PLA with an opportunity to gain greater experience and practice in interoperating with more experienced armed forces on the battlefield.[23] But within a Central Asian context, it has provided an environment in which Chinese forces have worked closely with their counterparts in countries where Chinese security concerns are fairly acute. For example, while most SCO exercises involve multiple actors across the region, with Kyrgyzstan and Tajikistan, China has undertaken specific bilateral exercises focused on counter-terrorism and border security.[24] This on top of a growing volume of gifts of equipment to security forces in both countries, including bases, regular support when they are due to host SCO summits, other more basic equipment (including radio and technical equipment which is provided both through grants and gifts from security forces, but also straight sales) highlights a growing relationship. At a normative level, through the SCO and other bilateral security engagements, China has also managed to increasingly influence regional powers to emulate their approach to online security and countering the spread of what they deem extremist messaging online.[25]

Finally, within the security space, China is also gradually growing the volume of higher end military sales that it is doing in the region. From purchasing equipment from the region, China has now started to undertake a range of higher level activities that are focused on providing arms and weaponry to regional powers.[26] This is most salient amongst the richer regional powers – with Chinese firms selling UAV platforms to Turkmenistan, Uzbekistan and Kazakhstan. With Uzbekistan, the sales have included a reported factory where the UAVs will be assembled in Central Asia.[27] In addition to this, China has reportedly sold missile systems to Turkmenistan and a growing volume of Chinese firms are present at the bi-annual KADEX security expo in Kazakhstan.[28] China is still a long way from displacing Russia as the traditional security provider in the region, but the in-roads in high end platforms suggests a range of future opportunities which favour China.

This brief pen portrait of China's relations with Central Asia illustrates the complex and comprehensive nature of Beijing's growing influence across the region. Far from being a power that is solely focused on one aspect of the relationship, Chinese firms, government and influence is stretching across Central Asia both in geographical and normative terms. This is a product in part of physical proximity which both gives China an easy springboard into the region, but also provides it with a particular interest in ensuring the region's prosperity. As illustrated before, China's interest in Central Asia stems primarily from the hoped for beneficial knock on effect that Central Asian prosperity will have on Xinjiang, helping bring prosperity and consequently stability to the region. By turning Urumqi into the gateway for Eurasia through the first of the Belt and Road routes, China is intimately binding itself to Central Asia (and beyond), while also creating prosperity and stability at home.

But while this is China's intention, it is not of course how it always plays out on the ground. There are consequences to this growth and influence on the ground which provide a sketch of some of the longer-term impacts of not only China in Central Asia, but the Belt and Road more broadly. In the author's analysis these are captured through seven broad headings.

The first and most visible impact of China's growing footprint in Central Asia is a growing number of Chinese nationals in the region. Given China's history with the region goes back decades, this means there is a cadre of Chinese living in Central Asia who have deeply ensconced themselves within local societies. These have been substantially supplemented through large numbers of Chinese workers who have come to deliver infrastructure projects, extractives fields, or work as managers for Chinese firms operating on the ground. These numbers have become so substantial that Central Asian countries have often chosen to restrict or control access, and there are regular reports of clashes between communities of Chinese and Central Asian workers on projects. Chinese companies often advise their Chinese labourers to stay on sites or avoid fraternizing with local communities.[29] This is in part a security consideration, but also a product of the potential clashes that are generated.

For Beijing this community presents a two-fold issue. On the one hand it provides a political dilemma – the large Chinese population becomes the face of China in the region and any clashes or tensions between them and the local communities becomes a flashpoint Beijing has to manage. But the community also presents a target for those seeking to strike China. This is most problematic when they become the targets of terrorist attacks (such as the bombing of the Chinese Embassy in Bishkek in May 2016, or earlier killings of diplomats in the city)[30], but also when they become embroiled in local instability or the targets of criminal networks. This is increasingly a community which feels that Beijing should be helping provide for their security, and China will in some cases struggle to be able to completely pass along all responsibility to local security actors. As was illustrated above, China provides a growing volume of security equipment and training to Central Asia, and in particular Kyrgyzstan and Tajikistan, countries where there is a growing volume of Chinese nationals and a weak local security capability.

This presents China with a dilemma – Beijing would rather locals managed their security problems and protected their nationals by themselves, but in the absence of effective local forces, China needs to find alternative potential solutions. This gives China an incentive and interest to take a greater interest in local security questions – something that in the Central Asian context is further accentuated by the fact that China's Uighur community has deep links across Central Asia as well, providing China with an additional layer of potential concern. Whether using its own forces, proxies or developing more private military firms, China is increasingly exploring new tools to deliver security on the ground. This highlights a growing concern that China will find as its belt and road presence around the world continues to grow.

The second, long-term impact of China's growing footprint in Central Asia is the growing volume of Central Asians who speak mandarin or have studied in China. As mentioned above, a growing number of middle-class families are sending their children to Chinese universities, taking advantage of scholarships or the practical benefits of having a child who is able to operate in the midst of the economic boom story that is happening in their region. This is further magnified at a governance level, where China has run training programmes for security officials at numerous levels as well as with key bureaus in Presidential administrations. All of this has increasingly created a growing cadre of middle class and ruling elite communities who have some connection with China.[31] This link is one which will undoubtedly re-shape thinking and orientation and will create a web of soft power connectivity or links that will change China's role and influence in the region in the longer-term. This will stretch across society, and in turn globally, increasing China's soft power influence around the world.

This brings on to the third impact, that of China increasingly displacing regional hegemon powers. As China becomes a more significant player in regions like Central Asia, it starts to displace the local historical hegemon. Within Central Asia this is Russia, and while Moscow remains the preeminent influential actor within the region (reflected in the fact that new leaders will still tend to make Moscow their first port of call following elevation amongst other indicators), it is clear that there is a gentle shift happening. It is visible through a re-wiring of the region's infrastructure, and the gradual growing influence that is visible from Beijing across the region. As this plays out, it not only changes the economic geography of the region, but also impacts the security and political relationships that the local government will look to as an important partner. Played out in the longer run this can lead to a competitive environment that can transform a country's outlook and perspective. Looking beyond Central Asia this can have a huge impact on other Belt and Road countries in institutions like the Commonwealth or across Africa where European powers have previously held sway and influence.

There is a downside to this from Beijing's perspective though, coming to the fourth impact, which is that as influence increases this means that countries will increasingly look to Beijing to resolve local clashes they are facing and unable to resolve themselves. Within Central Asia this means a growing push for China to play a more substantial role in Afghanistan, as well (potentially) as Beijing playing a broker role in clashes between Central Asian leaders. While China may stick to its narrative of non-interference in the internal affairs of others, there is a question about whether this is sustainable if you are the major economic actor in a country. Not only does it become important for your own interests to ensure you have some influence, but it also means that you find yourself obliged to play some sort of a role.

Another negative side of this expanded influence and presence on the ground is that Beijing and Chinese actors on the ground also become a target of local anger. This fifth impact can be both direct and indirect – for example, the attack on China's Embassy in Bishkek, or the attack on the Chinese consulate in Karachi are both examples of direct targeting of Chinese interests. But just as often as these attacks are attacking China directly, they can also be targeting China as a way of attacking the local government. As the local authorities' increasingly influential and powerful outside partner, China can be a useful proxy for locals eager to express their anger against local authorities but fearful of direct protest. Nationalist moods are often harnessed by authoritarian governments to justify their hold on power, but this means that when local protestors attack an outside presence like China under a similar veil, when in fact they are angry at the local government, it becomes harder for the local authority to react. This creates a tension between China and the local authorities which can both complicate the delivery of projects but also present a direct security problem. As China becomes a more prominent actor around the world, becoming a target of local anger is going to be an increasing issue in many different forms, often as a result of actions not by Chinese actors but local authorities they are partnering or working with.

Furthermore, Chinese actions and deals in third countries can in fact exacerbate the very problems that are behind local anger, coming to the sixth impact. In countries, like the Central Asian states, with dominant central authorities there is often a problem of locals feeling left out from the decision-making process around projects that are taking place in the environment around them. China's projects merely support this narrative and direction, being for the most part government-to-government projects funded through state-owned policy or commercial banks, and delivered by state-owned firms. And even private Chinese firms that are operating in third countries will find themselves delivering projects that by their scale tend to have some link to the local state apparatus.

Yet in these same countries, many local problems and conflicts will often emanate from tensions between the government and local communities. By China focusing its economic investment relationships through the capital city and central government authorities, Beijing may in fact be exacerbating intra-country tensions. Heavy Chinese investment in a region delivered with approval by the central government in that country may be perceived by those on the ground as merely another branch of a predatory and antagonistic central government whom they have long seen as an adversary. China will find itself in the cross-hairs of local anger, exacerbating local tensions as well as creating potential security risks to its investments and any workers deployed to deliver it. This has already been seen in parts of Kyrgyzstan, Kazakhstan and Tajikistan, but will undoubtedly become a major problem around the world given the fragile states with authoritarian leaderships where China often finds its Belt and Road investments going.

Finally, the seventh impact in the list is the narrative vision that China has managed to project under the Belt and Road within both Central Asia and beyond. By articulating an overriding foreign policy vision which aims to build trade and economics corridors emanating out from China in every direction which are focused on improving prosperity, growth and openness, China is rhetorically projecting a foreign policy vision which can in many ways be summed up as "making money together". This is not to make a value judgement on the reality of this vision, but by creating a narrative which can be summed up thus, China is producing a positive foreign policy vision for the world which few would disagree with. And to some degree this is reflected on the ground, where notwithstanding the various strands of anger that are illustrated in this article, very few in Central Asia would say that they do not want Chinese investment. They may be concerned about some of the consequences of it, but broadly speaking they are eager to receive the money and investment.

Normatively speaking this places China in a highly positive position on the world stage. Beijing can paint itself as a power which is broadly speaking promoting prosperity and opportunity around the world, with the underlying intention to increase stability through this prosperity. The realities around this may be questionable, but it is a fairly easy vision and concept for governments around the world to align themselves with. This plays in contrast to a current American administration that seems set on confrontation around the world, European and western powers who drive forwards democratizing agendas, or powers like Russia who aim through subversion to gain relevance and disrupt the global order. Through the Belt and Road, China can paint itself as the world's connector focused on prosperity and opportunity, and to some degree this is how the country is seen on the ground. People may read stories of debt-driven diplomacy or be concerned about local environmental or labour issues they feel, but they also do see the volume of investment coming into the country through China. This vision that China is able to project is hugely positive and confuses how third countries in turn react to it, and some of the broader trends in international relations. For example, in the current US–China clash that is taking place, for Belt and Road countries that are recipients of Chinese investment, it becomes more challenging to side with the United States when the American narrative is one of rejecting opportunity. While Washington is doing a great deal to change this, China has to some degree started out of the gate with an attractive narrative that complicates how countries will react.

All of this serves to illustrate some of the longer-term potential impacts of Chinese investment and influence under Belt and Road rubric. While some of these may at first blush appear more Central-Asia specific, the reality is that they are universal issues whose resonance may be the true long-term effect of Chinese investment. It is certainly the case that Central Asia as a region is more significant for China than some of the further flung countries captured under the Belt and Road (the tie to domestic stability in Xinjiang illustrates this most vividly), there are issues playing out in Central Asia which will provide something of a sketch of what might be coming further down the road around the world. China has long treated Central Asia as a testing ground for its broader foreign policy efforts, it is therefore hardly surprising that Xi Jinping's keynote vision similarly grows from a strategic effort that has long been playing out in the region.

ACKNOWLEDGEMENTS

The author is grateful for the support of Gabriella Marchione for her help in researching this article.

NOTES

1. H. E. Xi Jinping, 'Promote Friendship Between Our People and Work Together to Build a Bright Future'. *Ministry of Foreign Affairs of the People's Republic of China*, September 7, 2013; H. E. Xi Jinping, 'Speech by Chinese President Xi Jinping to Indonesian Parliament'. *ASEAN-China Center*, October 2, 2013.
2. Eleanor Albert, 'The Shanghai Cooperation Organization'. *Council on Foreign Relations*, October 14, 2015.
3. Liu Caiyu, 'Chinese Premier Calls for SCO Free Trade Zone'. *Global Times*, October 10, 2018.
4. 'SCO Development Bank: Prospects of the SCO Development Bank'. *CGTN*, June 6, 2018.
5. Author interviews in Bishkek and Osh, September 2012.
6. For example, the Kyrgyz have long sought to host the Development Bank HQ. 'Presence of SCO Development Bank's Head Office in Bishkek is Crucial for Kyrgyzstan: Atambayev'. *AKI Press*, June 24, 2016 or 'Kyrgyzstan Supports Establishment of SCO Development Bank - Minister of Finance Zhaparov'. *AKI Press*, May 22, 2012.
7. 'Presentation of China Development Bank and SCO Interbank Association at SCO Headquarters'. *SCO Press Release*, January 22, 2018. http://eng.sectsco.org/news/20180122/377285.html (accessed 4 June 2019).
8. Anatoliy A. Rozanov, *The Shanghai Cooperation Organisation and Central Asia's Security Challenges*. Geneva: The Geneva Centre for the Democratic Control of Armed Forces, 2013.
9. Roy Anthony Rogers, 'The Radicalisation of Xinjiang: Its Roots and Impact on Human Rights'. *Contemporary Chinese Political Economy and Strategic Relations*, July 1, 2018.
10. H.E. Wen Jiabao, 'Chinese Premier Wen Jiabao's Speech at Opening Session of Second China-Eurasia Expo'. *Ministry of Commerce People's Republic of China*, September 2, 2012.

11. Isabella Massa, 'Export Finance Activities by the Chinese Government'. *European Parliament*, September 23, 2011.
12. Marlene Laruelle, *China's Belt and the Road Initiative and its Impact in Central Asia.* Washington, DC: Central Asia Program, 2018.
13. Wang Jisi, 'China's Search for a Grand Strategy'. *Foreign Affairs* Vol. 90. Issue 2 (2011): 68–79.
14. Audrye Wong, 'China's Economic Statecraft Under Xi Jinping'. *Brookings*, January 22, 2019.
15. H. E. Xi Jinping, 'Promote Friendship Between Our People and Work Together to Build a Bright Future'; H. E. Xi Jinping, 'Speech by Chinese President Xi Jinping to Indonesian Parliament'.
16. Masuma Farooki, 'China's Mineral Sector and the Belt & Road Initiative'. *Strategic Dialogue on Sustainable Raw Materials for Europe*, March 2018.
17. Kseniya Otmakhova, 'The Belt and Road for All', *TUDelft*, January 2017.
18. Brenda Goh and Mariya Gordeyeva, 'Shuttered at Home, Cement Plants Bloom Along China's New Silk Road'. *Reuters*, January 30, 2019.
19. For example, most recently, 'China's Kazakh Ambassador Angrily Rejects Xinjiang Crackdown Allegations'. *RFE/RL*, May 28, 2019.
20. Author interviews in Urumqi and Shanghai in 2012 and 2014.
21. Bibolatova Akmaral, 'Shanghai Cooperation Organization – Reliable Defenders of Peace and Stability in the Region'. *People's Daily*, June 9, 2017.
22. Author interviews in Beijing November 2018.
23. Fabio Indeo, 'Russia-China Military Cooperation in Central Asia: A temporary Convergence of Strategic Interests'. *Italian Institute for International Political Studies*, December 21, 2018.
24. Le Tian and Jia Jieqiong, 'Infographic: A quick Guide to SCO and its Military Cooperation'. *CGTN*, June 5, 2018.
25. 'Statement by Heads of the Member States of the Shanghai Cooperation Organization on Joint Counteraction to International Terrorism'. *Signed Astana*, June 9, 2017.
26. 'China's Expanding Military Influence in Central Asia'. *Stratfor*, April 28, 2016.
27. W. J. Hennigan, 'A Fast Growing Club: Countries that Use Drones For Killing by Remote Control'. *LA Times*, February 22, 2016.
28. Joshua Kucera, 'Turkmenistan Shows Off New Chinese Rockets'. *Eurasianet*, April 2, 2016.
29. Author interviews in Kazakhstan 2012 and Turkmenistan 2014.
30. Olga Dzyubenko, 'Chinese Embassy in Kyrgyzstan hit by Suspected Suicide Car Bomb'. *Reuters*, August 30, 2016.
31. Author experiences during visits to Central Asia.

BEIJING'S RESPONSE TO THE BELT AND ROAD INITIATIVE'S "PUSHBACK": A STORY OF ASSESSMENT AND ADAPTATION

NADÈGE ROLLAND

Two speeches given by Xi Jinping in late 2013 – one in Kazakhstan, one in Indonesia – set the "Belt and Road Initiative" (BRI) in motion. What started as a continental Silk Road Economic Belt and a 21st century Maritime Silk Road embracing the Eurasian landmass from land and sea has since then expanded to include the African, South American and Oceanian continents, as well as the Arctic, space and cyberspace. The Belt and Road has become so ubiquitous in China's external discourse and practice that it is now almost impossible to distinguish it from Beijing's foreign policy.

Xi Jinping's plan has undoubtedly sparked a renewed global interest in infrastructure construction, but after five years of almost constant drum-beating, it looks like the BRI has recently reached its culminating point of success. A mounting wave of resistance against the BRI can be felt both within and outside of China. Some observers see it as evidence that the BRI is grinding to a halt, all the more so given Beijing is failing to understand and address the gravity of the situation.[1]

A careful reading of Chinese publications and examination of the inner workings of the BRI leads to another conclusion, however. The Chinese leadership is not oblivious to the gathering headwinds facing BRI. Rather, with the help of multiple actors, the Party-state system is assessing risks, tracking successes and failures, surveying local and international reactions, getting feedback, and recommending solutions. Based on this ongoing thorough assessment process, the Chinese leadership has decided on a recalibration of BRI's tactics. Observing how this process works reveals the existence of a sprawling system dedicated to making the BRI work and helps illuminate the Party-state's capacity to adjust and adapt.

The first section of this paper describes the domestic and international headwinds faced by the BRI. The second section focuses on China's response, analysing both the Party-state's assessment process and the content of the recalibration decided upon by the leadership.

Domestic and international headwinds facing the Belt and Road initiative

Resistance to Xi Jinping's plan to create a 21st century version of the Silk Roads appeared almost at the same time as it was launched, both domestically and internationally. A first wave of attentiveness and relative scepticism was followed by more pointed criticism as the years went by and as projects started to be undertaken on the ground. As Beijing accelerated its overseas push, foreign media reporting and academic analysis started to shed greater light on a series of projects undertaken under the Belt and Road banner and to denounce its intentions as well as its *modus operandi.*

Because of domestic censorship and control of public opinion, the level of resistance within China is difficult to assess, but there is evidence of a least a certain degree of disapproval from some public intellectuals. Internationally, several concerns have been publicly expressed by journalists, scholars and government representatives regarding the BRI's political, economic and strategic liabilities. The following section will first examine the anxieties that have been expressed publicly within China, before turning to a description of the range of international concerns and behaviours that comprise the recent pushback against BRI.

Domestic anxieties

The BRI is personal to Xi Jinping.[2] Sources in China hint that Xi personally supervised planning with a small group of close advisers before his elevation to the post of general secretary of the Chinese Communist Party in November 2012.[3] All major statements related to BRI have been made by Xi himself and, much like his association with the "China Dream" or the anti-corruption campaign, his personal identification with the initiative is incontestable. The consolidated position of Xi as head of the Party, the state and the military, as well as the system's "core" leader on a par with Mao Zedong and Deng Xiaoping, makes it almost impossible for anyone in China to challenge the wisdom of his decisions. The BRI appears to be no exception.

Yet, in the early years after the launch of the initiative, a few Chinese intellectuals dared to speak truth to power and offered words of caution.[4] Shi Yinhong, a professor at Renmin University, warned for example that BRI might be opening "too many battlefields" and over-stretching China's capacities; he therefore called for "strategic prudence," a theme resonating with Deng Xiaoping's long standing admonition to "bide time" as long as China was too weak to openly assert a great power posture.[5] Xue Li, from the Chinese Academy of Social Sciences, cautioned that if implemented hastily, BRI projects could become incomplete and be dismissed as "white elephants."[6] Such loss-making "face projects," conducted with limited transparency and oversight, are often seen in China as primarily intended to "reflect glory upon one's superiors" and disproportionately benefitting a handful of "connected insiders."[7]

As the BRI was about to celebrate its fifth anniversary in 2018, the concerns voiced by Chinese officials and academics focused more specifically on economic risks. During a Shanghai forum in June 2018, Hu Xiaolian, the Chairwoman of China's Eximbank, called on Chinese financial institutions to exercise caution regarding how much they lend to Belt and Road countries, and urged them to make sure to get their money back in the context of "uncertain international conditions with lots of economic risks and large fluctuations for interest rates in newly-emerged markets." Failure to manage those risks would mean increased financial difficulties for Chinese companies and for Belt and Road countries.[8]

A few weeks later, as Xi Jinping was about to begin a series of official visits to Senegal, Rwanda, South Africa and the United Arab Emirates, Sun Wenguang, a retired Shandong University professor, published a short letter criticizing the leadership for offering "almost 400 billion yuan in aid to 166 countries" (approximately $60 bn), an approach he characterized as "throwing money around." Meanwhile, Sun complained, China remained a country where the poor still struggled to pay for school, healthcare and support for their elders.[9] A similar critique came from Tsinghua professor Xu Zhangrun in a lengthy essay published online that offered words of warning to the Chinese leadership on a wide range of political and social topics. In particular, Xu criticized the government for excessive international aid. Commenting on "billions of US dollars" spent in Arab countries, he wrote: "Everyone knows full well that the Gulf States are literally oozing with wealth. Why is China, a country with over one hundred million people who are still living below the poverty line, playing at being the flashy big-spender?"[10]

Publicly-expressed domestic concerns are thus mainly related to sensitivities about the damage BRI could bring to China, in the form of a possible overstretch of the country's capacities and of what is perceived as overspending abroad to the detriment of the Chinese population.

International pushback

From the moment it was announced in late 2013, the BRI has also faced some resistance emanating from outside of China, which has evolved from scepticism, to suspicion, to opposition and counter-response.

In the early phase of the BRI launch, most countries around the world adopted a wait-and-see approach and tried to simply understand the initiative. BRI appeared both ill-defined and extremely ambitious, and individual countries needed to evaluate its possible risks and opportunities, as well as ponder its potential impact on their national interests. Much of the Western commentary at the time was sceptical of China's capacity to afford the immense cost of infrastructure needs in Eurasia in light of its own economic problems.[11] Some were openly suspicious of Beijing's intentions and expressed concerns about underlying geopolitical motives, cautioning that BRI, "the largest programme of economic diplomacy since the US-led Marshall Plan for post-war reconstruction in Europe," was helping China to set on a "road to empire."[12] In October 2017, US Secretary of Defence James Mattis commented on BRI during a hearing before the Senate Armed Services Committee: "There are many belts and many roads, and no one nation should put itself into a position of dictating 'One Belt, One Road.'"[13] Echoing the same idea during his official visit to China in January 2018, French president Emmanuel Macron warned: "These roads cannot be those of a new hegemony, which would transform those that they cross into vassals."[14] Malaysia's Prime Minister Mahatir bin Mohamad also appeared to express doubts about Beijing's real intentions when, during a press conference in August 2018, he commented that "free trade should also be fair trade", adding there should not be a situation where "there is a new version of colonialism happening because poor countries are unable to compete with rich countries." Mahatir's comments were then interpreted as leading the charge against China amid rising concerns about BRI's practices. In an interview with the BBC a few months later however, the Malaysian leader said this was an inaccurate portrayal of his comments.[15]

As BRI began to make progress in various countries and a series of controversial projects came to light, international criticism became more focused on China's dubious practices and the initiative's negative impact on local countries. Mounting evidence of problems with some BRI deals lent credence to what were until then mostly speculative readings of Beijing's intentions as being aimed at an expansion of its strategic foothold and geopolitical influence rather than merely developing regional trade. In early 2017, Brahma Chellaney, a professor of strategic studies at the New Delhi's Center for Policy Research, described BRI as a way for the Chinese leadership to use economic tools to advance their country's geostrategic interests. Through Belt and Road infrastructure projects, he argued, Beijing intended to ensnare strategically-located developing countries "in a debt trap that leaves them vulnerable to China's influence." Taking Sri Lanka's Mattala Rajapaksa International airport and Hambantota Port as illustrations of his broader point, Chellaney denounced China's overseas infrastructure ventures as

> intended not to support the local economy, but to facilitate Chinese access to natural resources, or to open the market for its low-cost and shoddy export goods. In many cases, China even sends its own construction workers, minimizing the number of local jobs that are created.[16]

Echoing the same criticism, US Secretary of State Rex Tillerson in October 2017 described China's model of financing infrastructure projects as "predatory economics" resulting in "financing default and conversion of debt into equity."[17]

The "loan-to-own" character of some BRI projects came fully to light in December 2017 when China acquired the Hambantota Port for 99 years after Sri Lanka failed to repay the loans that had funded its construction. In September 2018, following in the footsteps of Sri Lanka, Zambia handed over control of its international airport as well as a state power company because it too could not service its debt to China.[18]

As other similar examples emerged, more observers expressed concerns about increased vulnerabilities due to unbearable levels of debt owed to

China. In March 2018, a report from the Centre for Global Development warned that 23 of the 68 Belt and Road countries were "significantly or highly vulnerable to debt distress," of which eight – Djibouti, Kyrgyzstan, Laos, the Maldives, Mongolia, Montenegro, Pakistan and Tajikistan – were particularly at risk. The authors underlined their concern that debt problems "will create an unfavourable degree of dependency on China as a creditor."[19] A few months later, the head of the Overseas Private Investment Corporation (OPIC), a US-government international finance development agency, accused China of purposefully plunging recipient countries into debt in order to "grab their assets" and to go after "their rare earths and minerals and things like that as collateral for their loans".[20] At the November 2018 Asia-Pacific Economic Cooperation (APEC) summit, without specifically mentioning China by name, US Vice-President Mike Pence encouraged regional countries to choose the "better option" of American financing: "We don't drown our partners in a sea of debt. We don't coerce or compromise your independence. We do not offer a constricting belt or a one-way road."[21]

BRI's standards appeared increasingly problematic. In May 2017, the European Union's 28 member states declined to sign a statement prepared by Beijing to mark the end of the Belt and Road international Forum because of a lack of guarantees regarding transparency, sustainability and tendering processes.[22] A year later, a report co-signed by twenty-seven out of 28 EU ambassadors in Beijing (with the exception of Hungary) condemned the BRI for hampering free trade, giving an unfair advantage to Chinese companies, and attempting to shape globalization to suit China's own interests.[23]

While the US and the EU started to push back against BRI's geostrategic aims and lack of compliance with good governance standards, an increasing number of recipient countries began to have second thoughts about the terms of deals signed with China and expressed a willingness to go back to the negotiating table or even to cancel some of them, because of the unmanageable financial burden they would impose. For example, Indonesia and Thailand halted high-speed rail projects with China in 2015 (both countries ultimately went forward after Beijing adjusted its financial terms), Nepal cancelled two hydroelectric dam projects, Pakistan put a stop to the US$14 billion Diamer-Bhasha dam project due to "unacceptable" funding conditions, and the government of Sierra Leone cancelled the China-funded Mamamah International Airport project.[24] In May 2018, Mahatir announced his intention to renegotiate Malaysia's contracts with China, describing them as "unequal treaties." The Maldives and Myanmar also began to reconsider the scale and scope of their infrastructure cooperation with China.

The rising tide of concerns prompted discussions about possible counter-responses, focusing on alternative infrastructure development funding options, either unilateral or in conjunction with other countries. The US increased OPIC's portfolio cap from US$30 billion to US$60 billion and passed the "Better Utilisation of Investments Leading to Development Act of 2018" (BUILD Act) which gives OPIC authority to purchase equity in development projects, instead of merely providing loans.[25] Concomitantly, the US started to work in cooperation with other regional powers, notably Japan, Australia and India, to promote joint finance development projects in the Indo-Pacific region. During the 2018 APEC summit, Vice-President Pence announced for example that the US would help Australia develop a naval base in Papua New Guinea, and work with New Zealand, Japan and Australia to contribute to the development of Papua New Guinea's electrical power-grid.[26] India and Japan announced the launch of a joint Asia-Africa Growth Corridor (AAGC) a few days after the Belt and Road Forum in May 2017.[27] The EU released its strategy for connecting Europe and Asia in September 2018.[28]

Domestic and international opposition to the BRI has thus mounted in the five years since Xi Jinping announced its start. Several governments that were initially enthusiastic about Chinese investment want to revisit the terms of their deals, and great powers in Europe and the Indo-Asia-Pacific have launched a series of alternative options to counter the BRI. The list of examples of pushback may give the impression that BRI is now in a difficult position. However, the situation is not static. All of the countries that either cancelled projects or asked for a renegotiation of the contract terms still continue to cooperate with China under the BRI framework. Myanmar cancelled a dam project, but completed two China-funded pipelines, and went ahead with a more modest version of the Kyaukpyu port development project. Nepal cancelled two hydroelectric dams but the new pro-Chinese government restored one of them and added a railway construction project. Malaysia and the Maldives asked to renegotiate or review some projects, but also promised to remain part of BRI.

China's response: assessment and adaptation

Since Xi Jinping became Secretary General of the Chinese Communist Party in 2012, he has grasped all the levers of power in the Party and the state, in effect dismantling the collective leadership system and taking China back to personalistic leadership.[29] For some observers, this reversion to supreme personal authority risks creating a system that is "less agile and adept," less capable of adapting, more rigid, "inefficient, ineffective and brittle."[30] Because of Xi's anti-corruption campaign, bureaucrats appear paralyzed by fear of harsh punishment.[31] Those supposed to provide advice to the leader may be willing to align with his views and refrain from speaking truth to power, notwithstanding the reality of issues at stakes. Under such circumstances, China may risk lapsing into what Edward Luttwak has described as "great state autism," a condition in which Chinese leaders are incapable of clearly apprehending international realities, including mounting resistance to their own actions.[32]

As this section will show, a wide pool of Chinese regional and technical experts have been assigned the task of tracking and assessing the progress of BRI. Their work evidently is passed up to top leadership groups that have been established to supervise the implementation of BRI, culminating with Xi Jinping himself. In response to their assessment and perceived concerns, Xi has begun to announce adjustments in the BRI tactics.

Attuned: Taking the Pulse

In the months following the BRI's public launch, Chinese policy analysts started to examine the possible hurdles that could emerge and crafted a set of recommendations to address them. They based their assessment on their regional expertise, as well as on field surveys they conducted as part of research groups dispatched to several countries to probe local reactions to the Chinese plan. The sum of their collective work identified a set of challenges that could hamper BRI's success.[33]

The first had to do with China's lack of experience and knowledge of the socio-political complexities of countries traversed by the Belt and Road. The experts cautioned that it would take a while for Chinese businesses venturing out into Belt and Road countries to fully understand and efficiently operate in unfamiliar environments. Their lack of experience could cause them to make mistakes. In addition, local insurgents or terrorist groups could put the security of the projects and personnel at risk. BRI's economic viability and sustainability was another potential hurdle they identified. Experts discussed options for China to mitigate the financial risks, including spreading the burden among various international actors and institutions. Another anticipated stumbling block was the possibility of negative reactions worldwide to the initiative.

Other great powers might consider BRI as a threat to their own influence and would therefore try to undermine or oppose it. Smaller recipient countries would be uneasy about China's growing influence, and changes of government due to election cycles or local political instability could shift their attitudes towards BRI. In light of the events described in the first section of this paper, this assessment of the possibility of push-back looks prescient and mostly on the mark. The current resistance against BRI did not come as a surprise; it was anticipated.

The BRI risk-assessment did not stop in its early phase. It is an ongoing process, in which various entities deliver analysis and feedback to the central authorities which in turn provide guidelines, in what looks like an infinite loop. Although Chinese businesses and banks are undoubtedly involved in the technical assessment of various projects, their outputs are not publicly available. The following section will therefore draw mainly on the publications of regional and thematic experts from Chinese academia and think-tanks.

The Chinese Communist Party's top leadership supports the BRI assessment work undertaken by Chinese regional experts. In a speech made at the Warsaw Silk Road Forum in June 2016 Xi Jinping enjoined the think-tanks to play a "leading role" in advancing the BRI, to serve as "advisers and assistants for the government" in planning policies and designing appropriate mechanisms, and as "bridges" between the political level and the public opinion.[34] The vast majority of Chinese think-tanks and research centres are affiliated with either State or Party organs and their work directly informs and feeds the decision-making of the entities to which they belong. They also benefit from public sponsorship for research projects that are relevant to the political leadership's interests. For the year 2018, the National Social Science Fund of China provided grants for over 3,500 year-long research projects, 88 of which look specifically at the advancement of the BRI. Among the topics included are: "Corporate social responsibility in the construction of the Belt and Road," "The hedging effect of the US Indo-Pacific strategy on Belt and Road", "Winning hearts and minds along the Belt and Road in Southeast Asia", and "Populism risks along the Belt and Road".[35]

Think-tank experts and academics are expected to write articles, op-eds and reports that carefully study BRI's progress and problems, and to offer policy recommendations. For example, Zhao Lei, a professor of International Strategy at the Central Party School affiliated to the Chinese Communist Party Central Committee, identified several trends in the international "negative evaluation" of the BRI and in response recommended the creation of a grading mechanism for Chinese firms involved in BRI projects and a recalibration of BRI's activities. Instead of prioritizing "hard and heavy" projects such as ports and dams, Zhao advocated promoting "soft" projects such as education and training that could help to polish the initiative's positive image.[36] In an exceptionally detailed study of BRI published in 2017, Li Ziguo, a senior fellow working at the ministry of foreign affairs-affiliated China Institute for International Studies (CIIS), described both the success and problems encountered so far by BRI. Li identified a wide array of challenges, including security and economic risks as well as varying degrees of hostility towards China's projects. In response, he advocated preventive solutions: making a conscious effort to understand the recipient countries' demands and needs, learning to empathize with the locals' perspectives, creating a formal internal feedback and lessons-learned mechanism, and nurturing a talent pool of experts who can help with the risk assessment process. Zhao Minghao, a senior fellow at the China Center for Contemporary World Studies, (CCCWS) which serves as the in-house think-tank for the International Liaison Department, recommended that China plan "a positive, smart and prudent response" to the increased great power "balancing" against the BRI. This should consist mainly of cooperating, wherever possible, especially with businesses from countries that happen to be the most resistant to BRI (the US, Japan and India) in the hope that tough attitudes would then be softened.[37]

In December 2018, Peking University and the Beijing-based Taihe Institute jointly published an updated version of the "Five Connectivity Index Report" which evaluates the advancement of BRI in each of the "five links" that make up the BRI: policy coordination, infrastructure building, trade, financial integration and people-to-people exchanges. The authors of the report created mathematical formulas to process quantitative data from various Chinese and non-Chinese sources (such as the World Bank and the International Monetary Fund). The resulting scores helped rank the countries according to their level of performance in each of the five "links." A total of 11 countries ranked in the "smooth" category, while 21 belonged to the "connected" category, 30 to the "good" category, 21 to the "having some potential" category and 11 to the "weak" category. Russia, with a score of 86.24 points, topped the list, followed by Singapore (79.94), Malaysia (74.59), and Kazakhstan (74.52). At the very bottom of the list can be found the Cook Islands (25.90), Palestine (31.79), and Yemen (34.78). The report underlined the wide range of BRI's advancement level and, by identifying the shortcomings that need to be improved in each of the 94 countries studied, hoped to help address the problems "before they occur".[38]

Top-of-the-chain instructions

The Party-State has not radically altered the structure of its bureaucracy to adapt specifically to the needs of the BRI, but two central *ad-hoc* task-forces were created in March 2015 under the State Council's purview in order to supervise all the BRI-related activities: the "Leading small group on advancing the construction of the Belt and Road", and its subsidiary, the "Office of the leading small group on advancing the construction of the Belt and Road", located within the National Development and Reform Commission (NDRC) which manages the day-to-day central oversight and coordination work with relevant ministries and entities. A "Belt and Road Promotion Center" was added in 2017 within the NDRC's Office. It fulfils a strategic planning mission, which includes, among other tasks, the "analysis and assessment of relevant countries' political and economic situations."[39]

The Leading small group presumably meets on a regular basis, but its sessions are not necessarily announced publicly. Since a new team led by Vice-Premier and Politburo Standing Committee member Han Zheng was appointed in March 2018, the Leading small group has met at least twice: on May 25, 2018 and January 31, 2019.[40] During the same period, the Office of the Leading Small Group has also met at least twice: on 5 July 2018 and 27 December 2018.[41]

BRI Leading small groups have also been created in relevant Chinese ministries, such as the Ministry of Transport which hosted a meeting in June 2018 to review the progress made so far and plan for the next phase. Representatives of the State Railway Administration, the Civil Aviation Administration and the State Postal Bureau were present at the meeting.[42] Each Chinese province has also set up a local replica of the central BRI Leading small group. Similarly to the central one, groups meet on a regular basis and include representatives from a variety of relevant government entities whose responsibilities pertain to the advancement of the BRI. For example, in January 2018, the meeting of the Sichuan provincial office of the Leading small group involved officials from the province's Development and Reform Commission, Finance department, Commerce department, Foreign affairs office, Information and Technology commission, as well as the local branch of the People's Bank.[43] Detailed accounts of the above-mentioned meetings are not public, but available information indicates that their purpose is both to examine the tasks already accomplished and to plan work for the upcoming phase: in other words, to provide assessment and feedback, and lay out the next steps.

Thanks to the duplication of BRI Leading small groups at intermediary levels of the bureaucracy, information gets circulated both from the bottom-up and the top-down. At the top of the chain, Xi Jinping himself gives guidelines during regular study sessions specifically dedicated to the BRI (such as the Politburo sessions in 5 December 2014, 29 April 2016 and 27 September 2016) or uses important events such as the Central Committee 5the Plenary session (29 October 2016) or the 19th Party Congress (18 October 2017) to deliver important messages regarding the initiative.[44] On 27 August 2018 Xi chaired a symposium to mark the fifth anniversary of the launch of the BRI, which gathered all the domestic elements essential to the smooth implementation of his instructions: leaders of provinces, districts and municipalities, representatives from business companies, experts and scholars, as well as officials from the Central Commission for Discipline Inspection and the Supreme Court.[45] To ensure maximum circulation to the entire country, the meeting was widely covered by Chinese media outlets.[46]

Adaptive: From "Bold Brushstrokes" to "Detailed Painting"

The feedback loop, fuelled by the input of various domestic entities, allows the leadership to grasp better the challenges faced by BRI and to prepare counter-responses. In the face of the pushback against the BRI, the Chinese political system is not petrified, but rather adaptive and eager to "effectively respond to challenges brought about by changes in the external environment."[47] During the August 2018 symposium, Xi Jinping himself described this adaptation process as evolving from the bold strokes of a Chinese freehand painting style called *xieyi* to the more carefully-traced sharp details of the *gongbi* style.

As examined in the beginning of this paper, the main resistance to BRI during the first years following its launch was based on a negative reading of Beijing's geostrategic motives. The Chinese leadership fiercely rejects this view, and, with the assistance of the propaganda apparatus, they have spared no effort to try to downplay BRI's geopolitics. Xi Jinping has reiterated on several occasions that Belt and Road is "not a solo" performed by China but "a chorus" including all countries along the routes.[48] During the August 2018 high-level symposium, Xi insisted once again that BRI is "an initiative for economic cooperation, instead of a geopolitical alliance or military league, is an open and inclusive process rather than an exclusive bloc or 'China club'".[49] Foreign minister Wang Yi also rejected comparisons between the BRI and the Marshall Plan, and insisted that it was "not a geostrategic concept".[50] The same theme has been echoed in various Chinese state media outlets, including the *China Daily* insert in the British newspaper *The Telegraph* dated May 24, 2017, where the author, Dan Steinbock, a visiting fellow at the Shanghai Institutes for International Studies, wrote: "Unlike the Marshall Plan, the B&R does not predicate participation on membership or tacit support of military alliances. It is focused on 21st-century economic development, not the 20th-century Cold War".

In response to foreign claims of geostrategic intent, China is not trying to change BRI's intrinsic objectives, but rather to shape foreign perceptions in a more favourable way. Winning hearts and minds has become one of the priorities given by Xi Jinping during the August 2018 symposium. He instructed the propaganda apparatus to "optimize the contents and methods" of the propaganda campaign so that the people from the participating countries realize that the Belt and Road helps improve their daily life. He also urged winning over public opinion via the promotion of projects that "enhance the general populations' sense of real gain", insisting in particular on showing how BRI projects have helped with poverty alleviation and thereby ensuring that BRI will be "deeply rooted in the hearts of the people". People-to-people exchanges in the fields of education, science and technology, culture, and tourism are also to be promoted to help downplay the more strategic aspects of the initiative. Finally, Xi requested that more emphasis be placed on promoting the image of Belt and Road as a way to "improve the global development model and governance", and as a "powerful measure against unilateralism, isolationism, and against trade protectionism".[51]

Positive reinforcement of BRI is accompanied by an admonition to all the relevant Chinese entities to fulfil their responsibilities and take action to make it a success. Businesses and state-owned companies operating overseas must act as "Belt and Road ambassadors", making sure their behaviour and practices reflect well on projects that will be "worthy of praise". At home, there must be "no bystanders". The Party will strengthen its leadership and oversight, in particular as far as risk analysis and prevention is concerned, with the notable objective of refining the micro-analysis of various investment and construction projects in order to avoid as many pitfalls as possible.[52]

Finally, Xi requested that the initiative align more systematically with the needs of local countries. The process, usually described as “docking” in Chinese, consists in integrating the BRI within the participating countries’ own economic development strategies and finding synergies between what local governments want to get and what China has to offer. Whereas the first years focused on big infrastructure projects, Xi ordered that smaller projects, focused on high quality and efficiency, also be considered because they are expected to reinforce local popular support for the BRI. Each project ought to be “carefully crafted” so that each investment can “bring tangible benefits” to recipient countries.

Perspectives

In the face of the mounting international resistance against the Belt and Road Initiative, the Chinese leadership has proven capable of anticipating, assessing, and adapting to what looks like an increasingly adversarial environment. It remains to be seen whether and how the instructions given by Xi Jinping at the end of the Summer 2018 will translate into concrete amendments, but there are already indications that Beijing is willing to be more understanding about local constraints and more accommodating to the demands of recipient countries. In addition to infrastructure construction projects that are part of the China–Pakistan Economic Corridor, China has for example recently agreed to support projects in Pakistan that include water-filtering plants and healthcare.[53] The newly-created China International Development Cooperation Agency (CIDCA) will help cooperate in “softer” areas such as agriculture, education, and vocational training.[54] Malaysia’s Foreign Minister Saifuddin Abdullah indicated that China, cognizant of Kuala Lumpur’s constraint, was willing to reduce the size and cost of the East Coast Rail Link project.[55] A combination of aid and concessional loans might also help reduce the financial pressure felt by weaker countries.[56] Smaller, more financially manageable, welfare-oriented projects will not provide the same impetus as grand infrastructure projects such as the ones launched in the early phase of BRI, but in the longer term, they may help turn the headwinds back into Beijing’s favour. In parallel, Beijing will continue to push forward the projects deemed essential to China’s national interests.

Beyond tactical recalibration however, Beijing is unlikely to fundamentally alter BRI’s direction. The initiative is not just about building infrastructure or even sowing economic cooperation. Rather, as Xi made clear on countless occasions since the launch of his pet project, the BRI’s overarching objective is to bring forth a "community of shared destiny" which reflects Beijing's vision for a regional order centred around China – a concept enshrined in the PRC's constitution since March 2018. Bringing China back to its central position is the essence of what Xi called the "China Dream of the Great Rejuvenation of the Chinese Nation" and the BRI is the main instrument to help fulfil this vision.[57] As long as Xi Jinping stays in power, the chances that Beijing will scale back its ambitions and abandon the initiative are next to none.

NOTES

1. C. Balding, 'Why Democracies Are Turning Against Belt and Road'. *Foreign Affairs*, October 24, 2018, https://www.foreignaffairs.com/articles/china/2018-10-24/why-democracies-are-turning-against-belt-and-road (accessed 14 March 2019).
2. C. K. Johnson, 'President Xi's Belt and Road Initiative – A Practical Assessment of the Chinese Communist Party's Roadmap for China's Global Resurgence'. CSIS Report of the Freeman Clair in China Studies. March 2016. https://csis-prod.s3.amazonaws.com/s3fs-public/publication/160328_Johnson_PresidentXiJinping_Web.pdf (accessed 1 May 2019).
3. N. Rolland, *China's Eurasian Century – Political and Strategic Implications of the Belt and Road Initiative*. Seattle: NBR, 2017, p. 48.
4. Ibid., pp. 152–153.
5. Y. Shi, '"YidaiYilu": Qiyuan shenshen' [Belt and Road: Calling for Prudence]. Institute of World Economics and Politics, Chinese Academy of Social Sciences. July 30, 2015, http://ejournal.iwep.org.cn/index.php?optionid=979&method=letters&auto_id=2569 (accessed 1 May 2019).
6. L. Xue, 'Zhongguo "Yidai Yilu" zhanlüe miandui de waijiao fengxian' [Diplomatic Risks Facing the Belt and Road Strategy]. *Guoji Jingji Pinglun* Issue 2 (2015): 68–79.
7. M. Schrader, 'Domestic Criticism May Signal Shrunken Belt and Road Ambitions'. *China Brief* Vol. 18. Issue 14 (2018).
8. K. Bradsher, 'China Taps the Brakes on its Global Push for Influence'. *New York Times*, June 29, 2018, https://www.nytimes.com/2018/06/29/business/china-belt-and-road-slows.html (accessed 1 May 2019).
9. W. Sun, 'Chufang buyao dasabi' [Do Not Throw Money Around During Official Visits]. July 20, 2018. https://canyuwang.blogspot.com/2018/07/8.html (accessed 1 May 2019). Sun Wenguang was arrested on 1st August at his apartment while he was conducting an interview with the US-based Voice of America.
10. An English translation by Geremie R. Barmé of Xu's essay, 'Imminent Fears, Immediate Hopes' can be found here: http://chinaheritage.net/journal/imminent-fears-immediate-hopes-a-beijing-jeremiad/?lang=zh (accessed 1 May 2019).
11. See for example H. Broadman, 'Will China's "One Belt, One Road" Become a Bridge to Nowhere?'. *Forbes*, January 6, 2016, https://www.forbes.com/sites/

harrybroadman/2016/01/06/will-chinas-one-belt-one-road-become-a-bridge-to-nowhere/#7f12432d1f59 (accessed 1 May 2019).

12. C. Clover and L. Hornby, 'China's Great Game-Road to a New Empire'. *Financial Times*, October 12, 2015, https://www.ft.com/content/6e098274-587a-11e5-a28b-50226830d644 (accessed 1 May 2019).
13. United States Senate Committee on Armed Services Transcript on 'Political and Security Situation in Afghanistan'. October 3, 2017, https://www.armed-services.senate.gov/imo/media/doc/17-82_10-03-17.pdf (accessed 1 May 2019).
14. M. Rose, 'China's New "Silk Road" Cannot Be One-Way, France's Macron Says'. *Reuters*, January 8, 2018, https://www.reuters.com/article/us-china-france/chinasnew-silk-road-cannot-be-one-way-frances-macron-says-idUSKBN1EX0FU (accessed 1 May 2019).
15. B. Jaipragas, 'Is China's Belt and Road Colonialism? Mahatir: Not at All'. *South China Morning Post*, October 2, 2018, https://www.scmp.com/week-asia/politics/article/2166693/chinas-belt-and-road-colonialism-mahathir-not-all (accessed 1 May 2019).
16. B. Chellaney, 'China's Debt-Trap Diplomacy'. *Project Syndicate*, January 23, 2017, https://www.project-syndicate.org/commentary/china-one-belt-one-road-loans-debt-by-brahma-chellaney-2017-01?barrier=accesspaylog (accessed 1 May 2019).
17. 'US Supports India Stand on OBOR, Hits Out at China's Financing'. *Financial Express*, October 19, 2017, https://www.financialexpress.com/world-news/us-supports-india-stand-on-obor-hits-out-at-chinas-financing/899200/ (accessed 1 May 2019).
18. R. Krah, 'China to Take Over Zambia's International Airport for Debt'. *African Stand*, September 8, 2018, https://www.africanstand.com/news/africa/east-africa/china-to-take-over-zambias-international-airport-for-debt-repayment/ (accessed 1 May 2019); 'China to Take Over Zambia's State Power Company Over Unpaid Debt, Report Claims'. *Daily Sabah*, September 9, 2018, https://www.dailysabah.com/energy/2018/09/09/china-to-take-over-zambias-state-power-company-over-unpaid-debt-report-claims (accessed 1 May 2019).
19. J. Hurley, S. Morris, and G. Portelance, 'Examining the Debt Implications of the Belt and Road Initiative from a Policy Perspective'. *Center for Global Development* March 4, 2018, https://www.cgdev.org/publication/examining-debt-implications-belt-and-road-initiative-a-policy-perspective (accessed 1 May 2019).
20. O. Churchill, 'China Hasn't Changed Belt and Road's "Predatory Overseas Investment Model", US Official Says'. *South China Morning Post*, September 13, 2018, https://m.scmp.com/news/china/diplomacy/article/2163972/china-hasnt-changed-belt-and-roads-predatory-overseas (accessed 1 May 2019).
21. C. Yong, 'APEC Summit – Pence Warns Indo-Pacific Region Against China's Debt Diplomacy, Says US Offers "Better Option"'. *Straits Times*, November 17, 2018, https://www.straitstimes.com/world/united-states/pence-slms-china-says-us-offers-countries-better-option (accessed 1 May 2019).
22. T. Phillips, 'EU Backs Away from Trade Statement in Blow to China's "Modern Silk Road" Plan'. *Guardian*, 15 May 2017, https://www.theguardian.com/world/

2017/may/15/eu-china-summit-bejing-xi-jinping-belt-and-road (accessed 1 May 2019).
23. D. Heide et al., 'EU Ambassadors Band Together Against Silk Road'. *Handelsblatt*, April 17, 2018, https://www.handelsblatt.com/today/politics/china-first-eu-ambassadors-band-together-against-silk-road/23581860.html?ticket=ST-49154-aRpcF1xZtffQcbcCqSgg-ap4 (accessed 1 May 2019).
24. 'Mamamah Airport: Sierra Leone Cancels China-Funded Project'. *BBC*, October 10, 2018. https://www.bbc.com/news/world-africa-45809810 (accessed 1 May 2019).
25. S.I. Akhtar and C. Tarnoff, 'OPIC, USAID, and Proposed Development Finance Reorganization'. *Congressional Research Service*, April 27, 2018, https://fas.org/sgp/crs/row/R45180.pdf (accessed 1 May 2019).
26. 'US Allies Counter China with Alternative Electricity Plan for Papua New Guinea'. *Straits Times*, November 18, 2018, https://www.straitstimes.com/asia/us-allies-counter-china-with-alternative-electricity-plan-for-papua-new-guinea (accessed 1 May 2019).
27. J.P. Panda, 'Asia-Africa Growth Corridor- An India-Japan Arch in the Making?'. *Institute for Security and Development Policy*, August 2017, http://isdp.eu/publication/asia-africa-growth-corridor-aagc-india-japan/ (accessed 1 May 2019).
28. 'The European Way to Connectivity – A New Strategy on How to Better Connect Europe and Asia'. *European Union External Action*, September 19, 2018, https://eeas.europa.eu/headquarters/headquarters-Homepage/50752/european-way-connectivity—-new-strategy-how-better-connect-europe-and-asia_en (accessed 1 May 2019).
29. Susan Shirk, 'China in Xi's "New Era"- The Return to Personalistic Rule'. *Journal of Democracy* Vol. 29. Issue 2 (April 2018).
30. J. Tepperman, 'China's Great Leap Backward'. *Foreign Policy*, October 15, 2018, https://foreignpolicy.com/2018/10/15/chinas-great-leap-backward-xi-jinping/ (accessed 1 May 2019).
31. M. Pei, 'China's Rule of Fear'. *Huffington Post*, February 16, 2016, https://www.huffingtonpost.com/minxin-pei/china-rule-fear_b_9243774.html (accessed 1 May 2019).
32. Edward Luttwak, *The Rise of China vs. The Logic of Strategy*. Cambridge, MA: Belknap Press of Harvard University Press, 2012.
33. The following paragraph is a summary of N. Rolland, *China's Eurasian Century?*, pp. 151–175.
34. W. Li, 'Think Tanks Need to Play a Leading Role in Advancing the Belt and Road Initiative'. *Development Research Centre of the State Council of the People's Republic of China*, July 25, 2017, http://en.drc.gov.cn/2017-07/25/content_30242333.htm (accessed 1 May 2019).
35. '2018 nian guojia shehui kexue jijin lixiang mingdan' [List of National Social Science Funding 2018]. June 5, 2018, https://www.cingta.com/detail/5414 (accessed 1 May 2019).
36. L. Zhao, '"YidaiYilu" – Ruhe yingdui fumian pingjia?' ["Belt and Road" – How to Deal with the Negative Evaluation?]. *Chinese Financial Times*, July 23, 2018, http://www.ftchinese.com/story/001078585?full=y&archive (accessed 1 May 2019).

37. M. Zhao, 'Mei Ri Yin la "jijian pengyou quan", xiang gan ma?' [US, Japan, and India are Pulling a "Circle of Infrastructure Friends", What Should Be Done?]. *The Paper*, September 26, 2017, https://www.thepaper.cn/newsDetail_forward_1807019 (accessed 1 May 2019).
38. '"Yidai Yilu" wutong zhishu yanjiu baogao (2018) fabu' ["Belt and Road" Five Connectivity Index Published]. *Taihe Think-Tank*, December 26, 2018, http://brgg.fudan.edu.cn/articleinfo_440_3.html (accessed 1 May 2019).
39. 'Guojia fazhan he gaige weiyuanhui Yidai Yilu jianshe cujin zhongxin 2018 nian mianxiang shehui gongkai zhaopin gongzuo renyuan gonggao' [National Development and Reform Commission Belt and Road Construction Promotion Center, 2018 Staff Recruitment Public Announcement]. November 2, 2018. https://news.sina.com.cn/o/2018-11-06/doc-ihnknmqx6767007.shtml (accessed 1 May 2019).
40. 'Han Zheng zhuchi zhaokai tuijin "Yidai Yilu" jianshe gongzuo lingdao xiaozu huiyi' [Han Zheng Chairs Meeting of the Leading Small Group on Advancing the Construction of the "Belt and Road"]. *Guancha*, May 25, 2018, https://www.guancha.cn/politics/2018_05_25_457969.shtml (accessed 1 May 2019); 'Han Zheng chuxi tuijin "Yidai Yilu" jianshe gongzuo lingdao xiaozu huiyi' [Han Zheng Attends Meeting of the Leading Small Group on Advancing the Construction of the "Belt and Road"]. *Xinhua*, January 31, 2019, http://cpc.people.com.cn/n1/2019/0131/c64094-30603943.html (accessed 1 May 2019).
41. 'Tuijin "Yidai Yilu" jianshe gongzuo lingdao xiaozu bangongshi zhaokai bangongshi zhuren huiyi' [Office of the Leading Small Group on Advancing the Construction of the "Belt and Road" Convenes Office Directors Meeting]. *Sohu*, July 6, 2018, http://www.sohu.com/a/239601622_269004 (accessed 1 May 2019); 'Tuijin "Yidai Yilu" jianshe gongzuo lingdao xiaozu bangongshi zhaokai bangongshi zhuren huiyi' [Office of the Leading Small Group on Advancing the Construction of the "Belt and Road" Convenes Office Directors Meeting]. *Belt and Road Portal*, December 30, 2018, https://www.yidaiyilu.gov.cn/xwzx/bwdt/76105.htm (accessed 1 May 2019).
42. 'Li Xiaopeng zai bu tuijin "Yidai Yilu" jianshe gongzuo lingdao xiaozu huiyi shang qiangdiao: Fahui xianxing zuoyong gao zhiliang gao shuiping tuijin "Yidai Yilu" jianshe' [At the meeting of the ministerial small leading group on advancing the construction of the "Belt and Road" Li Xiaopeng stressed the need to play a leading role in high quality, high standard to build the "Belt and Road"] Ministry of Transport of the PRC. June 12, 2018, http://www.mot.gov.cn/jiaotongyaowen/201806/t20180612_3032318.html (accessed 1 May 2019).
43. 'Sichuan sheng tuijin "Yidai Yilu" jianshe gongzuo lingao xiaozu bangongshi zhaokai zhuanti huiyi' [Sichuan Province Office of the Leading Small Group on Advancing the "Belt and Road" Holds a Special Meeting]. *National Development and Reform Commission*, January 9, 2018, http://www.ndrc.gov.cn/dffgwdt/201801/t20180109_873301.html (accessed 1 May 2019).
44. '"Xi Jinping tan "Yidai Yilu"" zhuyao pianmu jieshao' [Introducing the Main Items of "Xi Jinping Discusses 'Belt and Road'"]. *People's Daily*, December 12, 2018, http://paper.people.com.cn/rmrb/html/2018-12/12/nw.D110000renmrb_20181212_1-02.htm (accessed 1 May 2019).

45. 'Xi Gives New Impetus to Belt and Road'. *Xinhua*, August 28, 2018, http://www.xinhuanet.com/english/2018-08/28/c_137423414.htm (accessed 1 May 2019). 'Xi Jinping: tuidong gongjian "Yidai Yilu" zoushen zoushi zaofu renmin' [Xi Jinping: Belt and Road Construction to Better Benefit the People]. *Xinhua*, August 27, 2018, http://cpc.people.com.cn/n1/2018/0827/c64094-30254137.html (accessed 1 May 2019).
46. H. Fan, 'Tuidong gong jian "Yidai Yilu" xiang gao zhiliang fazhan zhuanbian' [Promoting the Transformation of the "Belt and Road" to the High-Quality Development]. *People's Daily*, October 29, 2018, http://paper.people.com.cn/rmrb/html/2018-10/29/nw.D110000renmrb_20181029_1-07.htm (accessed 1 May 2019); 'Wu zhounian!"Yidai Yilu" zai chufa, Xi Jinping de zhexie tifa yiwei shenyuan' [Five Years! "Belt and Road's" Fresh Start, Xi Jinping's Instructions are Far-Reaching]. *China Daily* September 7, 2018, http://china.chinadaily.com.cn/2018-09/07/content_36879616.htm (accessed 1 May 2019); T. Pu, and Z. Bian, 'Cong "da xieyi" dao "gongbi hua": Liaojie "yidai yilu" zuixin guihua [From "Big Brushstrokes" to "Fine Painting": Understanding the Latest Plan for "Belt and Road"]'. *Qiushi*, August 28, 2018, http://www.qstheory.cn/zhuanqu/2018-08/28/c_1123340591.htm (accessed 1 May 2019).
47. D. Gitter et al., 'Party Watch Weekly Report 1.26-2.1.2019', https://www.ccpwatch.org/single-post/2019/02/01/Weekly-Report-216-1262019-212019 (accessed 1 May 2019).
48. 'Xi on Belt and Road : Not China's Solo But Inspiring Chorus'. *Xinhua*, March 28, 2015, http://china.org.cn/china/2015-03/28/content_35181785.htm (accessed 1 May 2019).
49. 'Xi Pledges to Bring Benefits to People Through Belt and Road Initiative'. *Xinhua*, August 27, 2018, http://www.xinhuanet.com/english/2018-08/28/c_137423397.htm (accessed 1 May 2019).
50. S. Zheng, 'China Embarks on Belt and Road Publicity Blitz after Malaysia Says No to Debt-Heavy Infrastructure Projects'. *South China Morning Post*, August 26, 2018, https://www.scmp.com/news/china/diplomacy-defence/article/2161418/china-embarks-belt-and-road-publicity-blitz-after (accessed 1 May 2019).
51. H. Fan, 'Tuidong gong jian "Yidai Yilu" xiang gao zhiliang fazhan zhuanbian' [Promoting the Transformation of the "Belt and Road" to the High-Quality Development]. *People's Daily*, October 29, 2018, http://paper.people.com.cn/rmrb/html/2018-10/29/nw.D110000renmrb_20181029_1-07.htm (accessed 1 May 2019).
52. Ibid.
53. Z. Baig, 'Chinese Government to Initiate Welfare Projects Along CPEC Routes'. *The Express Tribune*, February 12, 2019, https://tribune.com.pk/story/1908876/1-chinese-government-initiate-welfare-projects-along-cpec-routes/ (accessed 1 May 2019).
54. F. Yousafzai, 'China, Pakistan Set to Finalize Socio-Economic Development Action Plan'. *The Nation*, February 20, 2019, https://nation.com.pk/20-Feb-2019/china-pakistan-set-to-finalise-socio-economic-development-action-plan (accessed 1 May 2019).

55. A. Shukry and A. Raghu, 'Malaysia Nears Deal with China to Revive $20 Billion Rail'. *Bloomberg*, February 19, 2019, https://www.bloomberg.com/news/articles/2019-02-19/malaysia-nears-deal-with-china-to-revive-scrapped-rail-project (accessed 1 May 2019).
56. W. Song, 'Better Funding Mix to Help Clear Misreading of China's Engagement in Africa'. *Global Times*, November 7, 2018, http://www.globaltimes.cn/content/1126344.shtml (accessed 1 May 2019).
57. Rolland, *China's Eurasian Century*, op. cit.

THE CHINA-PAKISTAN ECONOMIC CORRIDOR: THE LURE OF EASY FINANCING AND THE PERILS OF POOR PLANNING

ARIF RAFIQ

Introduction

The China-Pakistan Economic Corridor (CPEC) is among the more advanced Belt and Road Initiative (BRI) projects, with $18.9 billion in CPEC projects initiated or completed as of December 2018.[1]

Given the close strategic ties between Beijing and Islamabad, and the popularity of China among Pakistanis, CPEC serves as a valuable BRI case study, providing insights into how the programme has operated in a country with limited initial political barriers to Chinese aid and investment. China and Pakistan have had robust diplomatic and defence relations since the late 1960s. Economic ties have, however, remained weak. CPEC marked the start of a venture into unchartered waters with respect to the bilateral relationship.

At the outset, when CPEC was formally launched in 2015, 82 per cent of Pakistanis had a favourable opinion of China, according to a poll by the Pew Global Attitudes Project.[2] The only country that had a more favourable opinion of China that year was China itself.

Given the strength of the strategic partnership, and favourable opinions of China in Pakistan – at least at the aggregate level – this was a unique starting point when compared to other BRI countries that have had a more ambivalent perspective on China. Many of the barriers to success in other BRI countries, such as long-standing anti-China sentiment or resentment of ethnic Chinese persons, do not exist in a prevalent form in Pakistan. But there have also been similar and unique barriers to the successful implementation of BRI in the Pakistani context, including corruption and political wrangling.

Four years since its formal launch, CPEC demonstrates the lure of easy financing from Beijing for developing economies and the perils of poor planning by recipient countries. In the short-term, CPEC has not served as the transformative force as which it was originally billed. Instead, it has exacerbated Pakistan's macroeconomic imbalances, contributing to a surge in the current account deficit and helping create another boom–bust economic cycle.

Objections over a lack of equitable geographical distribution of CPEC's projects in its early stage resulted in additions from smaller provinces, bloating the portfolio and weakening its coherence and economic viability. As it stands, CPEC is a series of energy and infrastructure projects without an anchoring, structured economic plan. To continue successfully, it will have to be retrofitted with one. Beijing and Islamabad are taking steps to retool CPEC as a vehicle for sustainable economic growth. But this is a difficult task for Pakistan in a phase of austerity and reform.

What is CPEC?

The China-Pakistan Economic Corridor is a connectivity project that aims to link Kashgar in China's landlocked western region of Xinjiang with Pakistan's Arabian Sea coast, an area home to two established ports – Karachi and Port Qasim – and the Chinese-operated port of Gwadar.[3]

The CPEC portfolio has been said to consist of projects totalling upwards of $62 billion in cost.[4] But this is a fluid figure. Pakistan may not have the capacity to absorb this entire amount of aid and investment. What is more salient is that the amount of aid and investment that has come into the country through CPEC is quite considerable.

Presently, $18.9 billion in CPEC projects have been initiated or completed, according to the Chinese Embassy in Islamabad. This figure includes two sets of coal-fired power plants that now provide electricity to the grid in Pakistan – both of which were completed in relatively short time.

Roughly 70 per cent of the potential CPEC expenditures are for electric power projects, most of which are coal-fired plants. Though they are regarded as private investment, there is an inter-governmental role. Sovereign guarantees have been provided for repayment. Pakistan has agreed to set up a "revolving fund" to ensure that at least 22 per cent of the estimated electric power charges are repaid to Chinese state-owned enterprises that serve as independent power producers supplying electricity to Pakistan's public utility companies.[5]

The idea is – or, at least, was – to address Pakistan's electric power deficit and inefficiencies in its ground infrastructure, paving the way for investments in the country's agricultural and industrial sectors. However, there have been complications along that road.

Punjab moves at the speed of China

CPEC is one of the more advanced Belt and Road-linked corridors, at least with respect to the total cost of initiated and completed projects. The $18.9 billion figure demonstrates that CPEC has also been an effective medium through which to fast-track the completion of infrastructure projects. The CPEC portfolio includes a few projects that have been on Pakistan's wish list for quite some time, going back to the 1990s. Pakistan had failed to push many of these projects forward because of the significant legal, political, and security risks the country poses to foreign investors. Also inhibiting investment is a colonial-era designed bureaucracy that is ill-equipped to serve as a facilitating or catalyzing force in today's global economy.

Through the ad-hoc CPEC bilateral framework, many projects were able to achieve financial closure and even become operational at a speed not typically associated with a country like Pakistan. Several of the projects have been completed much earlier than one would see in any country other than China.[6]

The major completed projects were launched and completed during the tenure of the previous government run by the Pakistan Muslim League – Nawaz party (PML-N). Several key projects were located in the PML-N-run Punjab Province, or even sponsored by the PML-N-run provincial government and personally directed by the chief minister, Shahbaz Sharif. And so a phrase was coined to characterize this rapid completion of projects: "Punjab speed." The inference was that the province of Punjab was able to match the speedy delivery that has been associated with infrastructure projects in China. So "China speed" had been matched by "Punjab speed."

CPEC was also a somewhat effective mechanism for Pakistan to overcome reputational disadvantages. From 2013 to 2015 – the period in which CPEC was initiated and launched – Pakistan had seen a resurgence of anti-state jihadist networks and was in the midst of a failed process of negotiations with the Tehreek-e Taliban Pakistan network. In mid-2014, the Pakistan Army launched Operation Zarb-e Azb. The year ended with the horrific school massacre in Peshawar. But since then, terrorist attacks have dropped precipitously each year, reaching their lowest levels in 15 years in 2018.[7] But in 2013, Pakistan was regarded as one of the world's most dangerous countries and few were willing to invest in it. So CPEC served as a critical morale booster for Pakistan.

Worsening the economic disequilibrium

Speed alone is not a meaningful benchmark for sustainable development. The primary motivation for "Punjab speed" was political. The Punjab-based PML-N sought to complete major energy infrastructure projects, including those through CPEC, before the 2018 general elections. The Pakistani economy, however, was unable to absorb this amount of investment in this short period of time, which required the import of heavy machinery. Pakistan is also a net energy importer. So along with the rise of crude oil and LNG prices from 2016 into mid-2018, CPEC-related imports widened Pakistan's current account deficit. Pakistan's forex reserves plunged, putting the country on the verge of a balance of payments crisis.

To avoid a balance of payments crisis, Pakistan is in talks with the IMF for a bailout. It has received or will receive short-term assistance from China, Saudi Arabia, and the United Arab Emirates. Pakistan is also attempting to pair short-term lending with foreign direct investment from these very sources.

The Pakistani economy, however, will once again slow. Public spending is being heavily cut. The rupee was devalued on several occasions in 2018. Interest rates and inflation are rising. Annual growth is estimated to slow over the short-term from a rate of close to six per cent in 2018 to around four per cent in the short term.[8] "Punjab speed" served as an accelerant to Pakistan's boom–bust cycles, which the country has seen repeatedly over the past few decades. This has prevented Pakistan from achieving long-term sustained growth as compared to regional countries like Bangladesh and India.

While CPEC gave momentum to a country where governance has largely been associated with lethargy, the lure of easy project financing also clouded decision-making, pulling Pakistan away from a path of responsible economic planning. In the immediate term, it has strengthened the disequilibrium in the Pakistani economy rather than serving as a transformative force.

Disincentivizing reform

Continuing with the question of transformation, CPEC may have also disincentivized reform – particularly in the power sector but also with respect to the judiciary.

Pakistan's previous government focused on ramping up power generation and reshaping the country's fuel mix, but once CPEC gained momentum, it lagged on combatting theft of electricity as well transmission and distribution losses in the grid. The grid itself still is unable to handle more than approximately 22,000 MW of electric power.[9] Energy sector reform, including dealing with liquidity problems in the power sector, has also stalled. Inter-company arrears within the electricity system continue to accumulate.[10] And Pakistan has struggled to pay some of the CPEC independent power producers whose projects are now supplying electricity to the grid.[11] As Pakistan's installed power generation capacity grows, so will the indirect liabilities of the Pakistani government, if nonpayment and losses from the grid continue at the same pace.

While power supplied through CPEC may bring down electric power price rates in Pakistan, it is more expensive or par with Pakistan's competitors, especially when factoring in the incentives or effective subsidies provided to Chinese companies.[12] Pakistani consumers will continue to struggle to afford the electricity offered to them. Pakistani electric supply companies will also continue to struggle to collect payment and arrears. Realistic pricing of electricity, keeping Pakistani income-levels in mind, is critical to electric-sector reform. Unfortunately, the previous government focused mainly on increasing installed capacity. And Chinese state-owned enterprises were focused on maximum profit generation, with guaranteed returns on investment of 30 per cent or more for many of these projects.[13]

Continuing with the subject of reform, much of the success of CPEC – and at least from a project management perspective – is due to *ad hoc* parallel structures created to facilitate Chinese aid and investment. But there is no major effort to reform the overall judicial system and improve the investment environment, especially when it comes to contract enforcement.

CPEC has addressed much to the uncertainty by doing away with open bidding, providing easy access to project financing, and enabling the redress of concerns and grievances through an *ad hoc* bilateral framework and offering Chinese companies informal, preferential access to Pakistani decision-makers. But for non-Chinese investors, Pakistan remains a market with a high degree of legal and political risk. This is why there has been an uptick in foreign direct investment (FDI) from China – at least from state-owned enterprises – but not sustained investment from elsewhere. There is now is likely to be a rise in FDI from Saudi Arabia and the United Arab Emirates, but the impetus for these investments may be geopolitics rather than domestic economic reforms.

Pakistan's (now former) Supreme Court Chief Justice had discussed creating an arbitration system for foreign investors similar to the system that exists in the UAE.[14] But political leaders have yet to initiate a dialogue let alone prepare legislation on such reforms.

Pakistani regulatory authorities have also weakened as a result of political and diplomatic pressure to push CPEC forward. It is these entities, such as the National Electric Power Regulatory Authority, that should be independent from external influence and improving their capacity and capabilities is key to improving overall governance in the county.

So as CPEC's fifth year begins, it can be said that the surge in Chinese investment has contributed to an economic bubble in Pakistan – and to prevent that bubble from bursting, the new government in Islamabad has little choice but to slow the economy, recalibrate spending priorities, and push forward systemic reforms.

It is important to keep in mind a longer term view when observing CPEC as well as the Belt and Road Intiative. Past is not necessarily prologue.

And if these long-delayed reforms are actually implemented over the next three to five years, CPEC could actually be identified as one of the contributing factors. While CPEC has induced what will be Pakistan's likely return to the IMF again later this year for the 22nd time in the country's history, as a result of direct pressure from the IMF and indirect coaxing from China, CPEC may also end up having induced Pakistan to take up electric power sector, regulatory, and taxation reforms previous governments deferred.

CPEC: A rudderless ship?

Moving ahead, CPEC will have to be retrofitted with an actual economic master plan. There is a CPEC "long-term" plan that was released in 2017. But it is largely a notional plan uninformed by a comprehensive feasibility study and forecasting. The CPEC long-term plan is an aspirational document that proposes three phases stretching over 15 years. It is now obvious that it does not guide decision-making by officials in China and Pakistan. Several developments make his clear.

First, there is no clarity on what is the firm basis for the inclusion or exclusion of projects from the CPEC portfolio. These factors are neither explicitly stated, nor can they always be inferred. For example, there are Chinese-funded electric power projects in Pakistan, such as a set of nuclear power reactors in Punjab and Sindh, that are not included as part of CPEC.[15] And there are road projects that are part of what Pakistan describes to be the CPEC road network, such as the M-8 Motorway, but they are not funded by China or managed through CPEC. In fact, some are wholly funded by the government of Pakistan. Ultimately, the question of what does it mean for a project to be included as part of CPEC has yet to be clearly answered. For example, municipal rail projects that have no relevance to a regional economic corridor are included as part of CPEC.

Secondly, industrialization is one of the main goals of CPEC, but rates for electricity produced by CPEC power plants are relatively high, despite the significant incentives being given to Chinese-state owned enterprises. This suggests that Beijing's goals to prop up troubled state-owned enterprises has been a priority over fuelling long-term growth in countries that receive Chinese aid and investment. Expensive energy will impede Pakistan's efforts to make its exports competitive and move away from an unsustainable import-based growth model.

Thirdly, there is a great deal of ambiguity and uncertainty surrounding overland Sino-Pakistan trade, despite the heavy expenditures. What type of future economic activity justifies the Pakistani government taking out upwards of $2 billion in loans to realign the Karakoram Highway, so that connects it to China? There is presently no investment from China in industrial centres that would leverage this connectivity in the coming years. Those funds would have been better spent improving connectivity with the Karachi area, which is home to Pakistan's two main ports. On account of budget cuts, the motorway connecting Pakistan's two largest cities, Karachi and Lahore, will be incomplete for the foreseeable future. While the Multan-Sukkur section of the motorway will be completed this year (through CPEC), the Hyderabad-Sukkur section that was to be funded by the government of Pakistan has been cancelled or delayed for now.[16]

Continuing on the issue of overland Sino-Pakistan connectivity, we speak of a China-Pakistan Economic Corridor, but we only know of the investments on the Pakistani side. What is being constructed on the Chinese side? And how will Pakistan be impacted by the internment of more than one million Uighur Muslims? Can this area, linked to Pakistan via the $2 billion upgraded KKH, really serve as a hub of regional economic activity?

Finally, there are no reliable figures on the projected impact of CPEC. The economist of Pakistan's planning commission during the previous government presented a fantastically absurd estimate of $6-8 billion in annual toll revenue and fees earned by Pakistan through CPEC.[17] He had estimated over $150 billion in China's global trade to be routed through CPEC by 2020. It is worth noting that in $80 billion in non-oil trade passed through the Jebel Ali Free Zone in 2017.[18]

The road ahead

For CPEC to succeed, the metrics for judging its progress will have to change. They are a means to peg government allocations toward concrete economic and development goals. Since its genesis, the main metric so far has been the size of CPEC: a project that began at $46 billion and then ballooned to $62 billion. Pakistani officials in the previous government had boasted about the growing size of the CPEC portfolio, though the growing size, through loans and indirect liabilities, also increased their challenges. Pakistan had effectively been competing with itself.

The true impact of CPEC should be determined by its impact on job creation, logistics efficiency, productivity, and exports. The present government in Islamabad appears to be retooling CPEC to some extent along these lines. But the opposition, including a minister from the previous government, have accused it of reducing the size of CPEC by cancelling or deferring some projects. Islamabad will have to resist the temptation to bloat CPEC with projects that lack an economic rationale right now.

CPEC will have to be retrofitted with an overarching plan that partly tries to leverage the infrastructure that has or will be coming on line. A year-long period to revisit and retune CPEC, as suggested by the new advisor to the Pakistani prime minister on trade, was a perfectly sensible suggestion.[19] But the idea was shot down because of opposition within Beijing and Islamabad.

However, China and Pakistan are taking steps to retool the CPEC framework. At the December meeting of the China-Pakistan Economic Corridor joint coordination committee or JCC, the two countries agreed that CPEC would now focus on agriculture, industrialization, and socio-economic development. In January, Prime Minister Imran Khan also included the Gwadar Port among CPEC's priorities going forward.

While all of these elements are more or less part of the original CPEC plan, they have taken precedence over initiating new electricity and infrastructure projects. There are two major reasons for this shift in emphasis: Pakistan's current account deficit woes and the Pakistan Tehreek-e Insaf emphasis on human development.

Beijing has also reportedly pledged $1 billion in development assistance over the next three years to Islamabad.[20] It goes unmentioned in a statement released by the Chinese embassy in Islamabad after the JCC. But the claim was made by a Balochistan provincial minister in December and unnamed officials in a Voice of America report.[21] If such a pledge has indeed been made, it would reflect Beijing's responsiveness to the priorities of the new government in Islamabad, which has placed human development and social service delivery above infrastructure.

While China has paired some of its investments in Pakistan's poorer regions with goodwill projects, these have largely been modest given the size of the two countries. Many or most of these projects have effectively been corporate social responsibility projects by Chinese state-owned companies. Beijing will now reportedly provide grants that cover "education, health, vocational training, drinking water and poverty alleviation projects." The programme could also include an anti-poverty pilot project.[22]

China can also share with Pakistan lessons from the ecological and environmental impact of its three decades of rapid economic growth. Climate change, deforestation, and water management are also on the joint working group's agenda. China has made major strides in recent years in reversing environmental degradation and adopting sustainable agricultural practices.[23]

A new set of agricultural projects are likely to be funded through the CPEC portfolio, including the channelization of an 180 km stretch of the Indus River in Sindh.[24] But for CPEC to transform Pakistan's agricultural sector, it will have to go far beyond large-scale irrigation projects.

At the December CPEC JCC meeting, China and Pakistan also signed a memorandum of understanding (MOU) on industrial cooperation.[25] The MOU identified textiles, materials, minerals, and petrochemicals as areas of focus. If investments in these areas do materialize, they would be through the CPEC special economic zones or SEZs.

The CPEC SEZs – most of which were proposed before CPEC was launched – continue to face the same difficulties as other Pakistani industrial zones. Most prominent among these are inadequate electricity and gas supplies.[26] According to the chairman of Pakistan's Board of Investment, none of the planned CPEC and non-CPEC SEZs have available more than 10 per cent of the electricity and gas supplies provisioned for them.[27] Pakistan continues to face natural gas shortages despite having secured several short-term and long-term LNG supply deals. Public sector mismanagement and corruption are rampant. Merely making the SEZs a priority will not resolve the problems with gas supply. Pakistan needs to be clear on exactly what purpose the SEZs serve. What is the distinct proposition that they offer as compared to investment elsewhere in Pakistan? What barriers to investment do they help overcome?

CPEC is far from the "debt trap" as critics claim. Like any large-scale public expenditures, it has been vulnerable to rent-seekers – including Chinese state-owned enterprises, competing Pakistani government ministries, as well as local politicians and politically-connected business barons in Pakistan. They have unmoored CPEC from its basic goal of enhancing connectivity and economic growth from western China into coastal Pakistan. To contain these rent-seeking forces, and for CPEC to serve as a catalyst for sustainable economic growth, it will require a structured plan for CPEC that ties future expenditures toward specific economic and development objectives and pushing forward systemic reforms in Pakistan. Given Pakistan's history, this is a radical proposition. But it is by no means impossible.

NOTES

1. 'Latest Progress on the CPEC'. *Embassy of the People's Republic of China in the Islamic Republic of Pakistan*, December 29, 2018, https://pk.chineseembassy.org/eng/zbgx/t1626097.htm (accessed 30 December 2018).
2. 'Global Indicators Database'. *Pew Research Center*, http://www.pewglobal.org/database/indicator/24/survey/all/ (accessed 30 December 2018).
3. 'Long Term Plan for China-Pakistan Economic Corridor'. *Government of Pakistan, Ministry of Planning, Development and Reform*, http://cpec.gov.pk/brain/public/uploads/documents/CPEC-LTP.pdf (accessed 30 December 2018).
4. Salman Siddiqui, 'CPEC Investment Pushed from $55b to $62b'. *The Express Tribune*, April 12, 2017, https://tribune.com.pk/story/1381733/cpec-investment-pushed-55b-62b/ (accessed 30 December 2018).
5. Khalid Mustafa, 'Delayed Payments Irritate Chinese Companies Working Under CPEC'. *The News*, December 19, 2018, https://www.thenews.com.pk/print/407726-delayed-payments-irritate-chinese-companies-working-under-cpec (accessed 30 December 2018).
6. 'Pakistan's Government is Fixing a Power Shortage'. *The Economist*, November 9, 2017, https://www.economist.com/asia/2017/11/09/pakistans-government-is-fixing-a-power-shortage (accessed 13 March 2019).
7. 'Fatalities in Terrorist Violence in Pakistan 2000–2019'. *South Asia Terrorism Portal*, https://www.satp.org/satporgtp/countries/pakistan/database/casualties.htm (accessed 13 March 2019).
8. 'Tighter Policies to Weight on Short-Term Growth in Pakistan'. *Fitch Solutions*, March 12, 2019, https://www.fitchsolutions.com/country-risk-sovereigns/economics/tighter-policies-weigh-short-term-growth-pakistan-12-03-2019 (accessed 13 March 2019).
9. Raha Rehman, 'Pakistan's Electricity Generation has Increased Over Time. So Why Do We Still Not Have Uninterrupted Supply?' *DAWN*, February 8, 2019, https://www.dawn.com/news/1430728 (accessed 13 March 2019).
10. 'Circular Debt Increasing by Rs1.27b Daily'. *The Express Tribune*, March 8, 2019, https://tribune.com.pk/story/1925238/1-circular-debt-increasing-rs1-27b-daily-ismail/ (accessed 13 March 2019).
11. Khaleeq Kiani, 'CPEC Consortia Run into Problems Over Payment Issues'. *DAWN*, June 21, 2018, https://www.dawn.com/news/1415110 (accessed 30 December 2018).

12. Arif Rafiq, 'The China-Pakistan Economic Corridor: Three Years Later'. *Reconnecting Asia*, February 12, 2018, https://reconnectingasia.csis.org/analysis/entries/cpec-at-three/ (accessed 30 December 2018).
13. Arif Rafiq, 'The China-Pakistan Economic Corridor: Barriers and Impact'. *U.S. Institute of Peace*, October 2017, https://www.usip.org/sites/default/files/2017-10/pw135-the-china-pakistan-economic-corridor.pdf (accessed 20 January 2019).
14. 'CJ Stresses Need to Revamp Laws for Quick Dispensation of Justice'. *DAWN*, December 12, 2018, https://www.dawn.com/news/1450838 (accessed 10 January 2019).
15. 'China Signs Deal to Build New Nuclear Reactor in Pakistan: WNN'. *Reuters*, November 24, 2017, https://www.reuters.com/article/us-pakistan-nuclear-china/china-signs-deal-to-build-new-nuclear-reactor-in-pakistan-wnn-idUSKBN1DO1W6 (accessed 20 January 2019).
16. Tahir Amin, 'Hyderabad-Sukkur Motorway: Project Shelved Due to Financial Constraints'. *Business Recorder*, December 24, 2018, https://fp.brecorder.com/2018/12/20181224433969/ (accessed 20 January 2019).
17. Drazen Jorgic, 'Pakistan's "Silk Road" Repayments to Peak at Around $5 Billion a Year: Chief Economist'. *Reuters*, May 10, 2017, https://www.reuters.com/article/us-pakistan-economy-china-silkroad/pakistans-silk-road-repayments-to-peak-at-around-5-billion-a-year-chief-economist-idUSKBN1861GH (accessed 11 December 2018).
18. 'Jafza Sees $83b in Trade in 2017'. *Gulf News*, May 15, 2018, https://gulfnews.com/business/jafza-sees-83b-in-trade-in-2017-1.2221977 (accessed 21 December 2018).
19. Jamil Anderlini, Henny Sender and Farhan Bokhari, 'Pakistan Rethinks its Role in Xi's Belt and Road Plan'. *Financial Times*, September 9, 2018, https://www.ft.com/content/d4a3e7f8-b282-11e8-99ca-68cf89602132 (accessed 21 December 2018).
20. Saleem Shahid, 'CPEC Body Approves $1bn Social Uplift Package'. *DAWN*, December 23, 2018, https://www.dawn.com/news/1453086 (accessed 30 December 2018).
21. Ayaz Gul, 'China Giving Pakistan $3.5 Billion in Loans, Grants'. *Voice of America*, February 15, 2019, https://www.voanews.com/a/china-giving-billions-to-pakistan-in-loans-grants/4788478.html (accessed 20 February 2019).
22. 'CPEC Economic Zones Will Help Bridge Trade Deficit of $9 b'. *The Express Tribune*, January 20, 2019, https://tribune.com.pk/story/1892885/1-cpec-economic-zones-will-help-bridge-trade-deficit-9b-khusro-bakhtiar/ (accessed 20 February 2019).
23. Brett Bryan and Lei Gao, 'What We Can Learn from China's Fight Against Environmental Ruin'. *The Conversation*, July 11, 2018, http://theconversation.com/what-we-can-learn-from-chinas-fight-against-environmental-ruin-99681 (accessed 30 December 2018).
24. 'Agriculture, Socio-economic Projects to be Made Part of CPEC: CM'. *The Express Tribune*, December 24, 2018, https://tribune.com.pk/story/1873254/1-agriculture-socio-economic-projects-made-part-cpec-cm/ (accessed 20 February 2019).
25. 'JCC Meeting: Pakistan, China Finalize MoU on Industrial Cooperation'. *The Express Tribune*, December 21, 2018, https://tribune.com.pk/story/1871431/2-jcc-

meeting-pakistan-china-finalise-mou-industrial-cooperation/ (accessed 20 February 2019).
26. Shakeel Ahmed, 'Power and Petroleum Divisions Have a Month to Submit Plan on Provision of Power and Gas to SEZs'. *Samaa News*, February 4, 2019, https://www.samaa.tv/news/2019/02/power-and-petroleum-divisions-have-a-month-to-submit-plan-on-provision-of-power-and-gas-to-sezs/ (accessed 20 February 2019).
27. Khaleeq Kiani, 'ECC Wants Expedited Utilities Provision at Special Economic Zones'. *DAWN*, February 5, 2019, https://www.dawn.com/news/1461930 (accessed 20 February 2019).

FLAWED BY DESIGN: THE CHALLENGE OF FLAWED DEMOCRACIES TO CHINA'S RISE

JAMES SCHWEMLEIN

Introduction

Much ink has been spilled about China's Belt & Road Initiative (BRI), President Xi Jinping's grand vision for leveraging China's growing wealth to expand economic, political, and military influence. The initiative is typically defined as encompassing projects in some 65 countries across three continents, and in sum it represents the greatest directed investment in history with an estimated value of over $1 trillion over the lifetime of the initiative.[1] But five years in, Xi's "project of the century" is facing turbulence – from indications that China's economy is slowing, routine construction and project management delays, and most interestingly efforts on the part of recipient countries to assert greater control over the direction of China's efforts.

Much attention has been paid to the notion of local challenges to China's BRI. But this commentary is misdirected. At this point, the issue is not an expansion of authoritarianism or the proliferation of a "China model."[2] Nor is it that local "pushback" marks emerging "resistance" to China's effort, or indeed to China's rise to great power status. Rather, what has been referred to as "pushback" or "resistance" should be understood narrowly as tactical efforts to amend, renegotiate, or cancel contracts or initiatives previously agreed and announced by Beijing and its local governmental partners. These signs need to be understood in more localized terms than they are typically applied. It is a mistake to confuse local efforts to assert greater influence or control over Chinese investments as a rebuke against China's rise to global power status. Individual states may choose to curtail or alter Chinese investment plans, but China will remain a large, potentially dominant, actor in most Asian markets, despite tactical challenges against some of its individual programmes.[3]

This article posits that incidents where recipient states have attempt to assert greater influence share a common characteristic – democracy. Or, to be more precise, partial or flawed democracy.

Of the 65 countries that have been identified as BRI beneficiaries since 2014, almost two thirds (41) are identified as either hybrid regimes[4] or flawed democracies[5] in the *Economist Intelligence Unit* 2018 Democracy Index.[6] Notably, no BRI beneficiary is identified as a "full democracy" in the EIU index.[7]

Of the 23 BRI beneficiaries identified by China that are characterized as authoritarian[8] in the EIU index, few have publicly sought to alter, renegotiate, or cancel contracts with China. Those who have appear to have made only limited adjustments. For example, Myanmar pressed to adjust the terms of lending for a large railway project in 2018, after it failed to meet growth expectations and deal with fallout of its handling of the Rohingya.[9] Difficult business climates, security concerns, and low governmental capacity among authoritarian regimes make project execution and management difficult. But none of the cases where authoritarian regimes were the local beneficiary of BRI investments have faced so-called "pushback."

This study will focus South and Southeast Asian states that fit the definition of flawed democracy or hybrid regime, are BRI beneficiaries, and had an election in 2017 or 2018 that produced a change of key political leadership, whether that be the head of government or head of state under the local constitution. Four cases fit this definition: Nepal, Malaysia, Pakistan, and The Maldives.[10] In each case, newly elected governments attempted to assert greater influence over the direction of China's efforts, with varying degrees of effectiveness.

Nepal

February 2018 produced a governing coalition led by Prime Minister K.P. Sharma Oli, whose Communist party entered into a coalition with its former rivals, the Maoist party, which earned the third most votes. Oli had previously served as Prime Minister in 2015-6, during which time he had signed the initial agreements to begin a range of projects with

China, including new roads, a railroad connection between Kathmandu and China, and two large dams. Oli's focus upon his election was first to modify the scope of the planned Chinese-built railroad to end the line at Kathmandu, in order to reduce cost and manage Indian concerns about the construction of a China-gauge railway up to its border[11], and second to attempt to insert a Nepali state-owned enterprise to lead development of a large hydropower project.[12]

Nepal's desire to accept Chinese investment was founded on two factors: a need for economic growth, and a desire to reduce its dependency on India for connectivity to the outside world as well as basic resources. Oli's re-election campaign was built around criticizing his two immediate successors, one from the Nepali Congress party and one from the Maoist party, for not effectively managing the implementation of the agreements he had signed with China.

The competitive dynamic between India and China is at the centre of challenges to China's projects in Nepal. India is Nepal's dominant trading partner, accounting for 63 per cent of all of Nepal's imports and 54 per cent of Nepal's exports.[13] India is also a necessary power source, exporting 1,400 megawatts of electricity each year to Nepal. While this dynamic of dependency led successive Nepali leaders to push for diversification, it also meant that New Delhi retained substantial influence. The presence of a dominant rival power was a complicating factor for China's efforts in Nepal.

The primary source of Sino-Nepali tension regarding BRI projects was in the hydropower sector. The development of two major dams was at the centre of Kathmandu's request to Beijing. The larger of the two, known as the Budhi Gandhaki dam, a 1,200-megawatt facility on the eponymous river just west of Kathmandu, was awarded via a government-to-government memorandum of understanding to a Chinese firm, Gezhouba Group Corporation. The smaller one, the 750-megawatt West Seti dam, was awarded by the same process to a subsidiary of the China Three Gorges Corporation. Both dams are viewed as vital to reducing Nepal's dependency on energy imports from India. China's financing was conditional on use of Chinese firms for the project, over Nepal's domestic state-owned power corporation, Nepal Electric Authority, for development.

China resisted local efforts to adjust the terms of the dam projects once they were awarded to Chinese firms. Successive governments attempted to renegotiate the terms of the Chinese financing to allow for the Nepal Electric Authority to serve as the lead project developer, but Beijing declined to adjust the terms. At the same time as it denied local requests, China was willing to alter terms for its own interests. Three Gorges cancelled its participation in the West Seti project in September 2018 over what were characterized as due-diligence related concerns about the potential costs related to displacing the local population.[14]

The case of Nepal exhibits relatively little challenge to Beijing's efforts under the BRI. Beijing entered into arrangements with the elected government, which were then challenged by successive governments. In Nepal's case, Ori's re-election to the prime ministerial position is indicative of the continuing vulnerability that flawed democracies have to elite capture. China's patience and persistence meant that it could literally wait out Nepali concerns and wait for a better answer. The harder challenge in Nepal's case likely will come from regional power relationships. India's persistent and dominant economic position in Nepal means that New Delhi could be disruptive to Chinese investments, over time. But China's focus on building direct road connectivity, including by allowing Nepal access to the Chinese market for the first time in 2019, means that India's primacy will be at risk of growing dilution over time.

Malaysia

Malaysia is one of the most prosperous states in the region. Unlike Nepal, its economy is heavily trade dependent, particularly because of its large oil and gas reserves. The state has a history of single-party dominance and is classified as a flawed democracy under the EIU's metric. But in May 2018, a decades-long stretch of single-party control was broken following competitive elections – albeit one led by a nonagenarian leader who himself has in the past served as Prime Minister for 29 consecutive years and can hardly be said to represent change.

Nonagenarian Prime Minister Mahathir Mohamed's break with his former party occurred as a direct result of allegations of corruption. China's robust financial commitments during the tenure of Mahathir's predecessor, Najib Razak, were at the centre of a tawdry web of financial wrongdoing. The lack of competitive procurement processes, the engagement of Chinese state-owned enterprises without participation of local firms, and concerns about the financial sustainability of the arrangements were at the centre of Mahathir's campaign.[15]

Shortly after taking office, Prime Minister Mahathir's announced that he would delay or cancel $23 billion in planned Chinese projects, including a high-speed rail line from Kuala Lumpur and Singapore, the East Coast Rail Link, which was to connect the east coast of Peninsular Malaysia with shipping routes in the west, and three pipelines. Then, during a dramatic five-day trip to China in August, Mahathir delivered what some read as a direct public rebuke of China during a joint press conference with Chinese Premier Li Keqiang in Beijing by expressing his concern over "a new version of colonialism." This is perhaps the strongest public rebuke to China's efforts from a leader of a BRI beneficiary.[16]

Malaysia is in a unique position among these cases, in that it is a highly differentiated economy, with numerous large trading partners. While China is Malaysia's largest export destination and source of imports, Malaysia also enjoys substantial trading relationships with Singapore, Japan, and the United States.[17]

But even Malaysia, with its comparatively confident economic position among BRI-recipient states, is not refusing financial support from China. Mahathir's careful focus on framing grievances domestically may have annoyed Beijing in the moment and fuelled international speculation, but the reorientation he sought is narrow. Mahathir used his bluster to push China to adjust project terms, reducing the financial costs and increasing the scope of local participation.[18] How and whether these measures are achieved are unclear at the time of this writing, but Mahathir was the first leader to confirm participation in the second BRI summit in April 2019.

Pakistan

Pakistan has been one the largest beneficiaries of Chinese investment under the BRI, with about $21 billion in projects achieving a financial close under the China–Pakistan Economic Corridor (CPEC) between 2014 and early 2019 and tens of billions of dollars' worth of additional projects under discussion. The overall effort, which is intended to be completed by 2030, straddle five sectors: energy, transportation, industrial production, the Gwadar port, and special economic zones. Initial projects focus on the energy sector, roads, and development of the Gwadar port.

The Pakistani politics of CPEC mirror other cases. China's surge of investment was initiated after a state visit by President Xi in April

2015. The project plans were developed in consultation with the sitting government at the time, led by three-time Prime Minister Nawaz Sharif, and projects were awarded via government-to-government memoranda of understanding, bypassing domestic procurement rules.

CPEC faced numerous challenges, and China and Pakistan adjusted course to try to compensate for local requirements. For example, China expressed concern about security threats to Chinese national staff in Pakistan, so the Pakistan Army created a stand-alone force of approximately 14,000 uniformed personnel responsible for providing security for CPEC projects, primarily in the restive Balochistan province. Two provinces, Sindh and Khyber-Pakhtunkhwa, which at the time were controlled by Sharif's rivals, claimed that projects had been allocated disproportionately to benefit areas that politically supported Sharif's party. China responded by publicly discussing a new series of transportation projects west of the Indus River path, which forms the primary artery of the state, and extended additional financial support for projects to develop local coal resources in the Thar desert, in eastern Sindh. The public discussion temporarily eased concern, though follow through has been slow on projects outside of the primary transport corridor.

What makes the Pakistan case unique is the depth of the pre-existing Sino-Pakistani relationship. Pakistan and China have enjoyed increasingly close military relations since 1971, when Pakistan fought and lost a war with India and, in the process, the country was cleaved in two, with the eastern territory becoming Bangladesh. China has provided valuable technological support to Pakistan's Army at several key moments, including in the development of Pakistan's nuclear weapons and ballistic missiles capabilities and more recently in developing a relatively low-cost fighter jet, the JF-17, through a co-manufacturing arrangement. CPEC marked the addition of a large economic component to a pre-existing, strong security and political relationship, which remains a stabilizing guarantee in the bilateral relationship.

As elections approached in 2018, opposition parties focused criticism on Sharif's handling of CPEC commitments from China. Three primary allegations became persistent: the procurement process allocating projects to Chinese firms; the role of Chinese firms in leading projects, effectively crowding out local competitors from financial benefit; and the allegedly unequal distribution of benefits among groups. Imran Khan's election as Prime Minister in August 2018 came as a direct result of these concerns, which were also reportedly shared within the military.

Shortly after Khan's election, a series of statements from senior Pakistani officials spurred tension with Beijing, including criticism that the Sharif government "did a bad job negotiating with Beijing,"[19] and an announcement that an $8 billion project loan to Pakistan Railways would be reduced.[20] While these statements drew attention, the Sharif government sought to shift China's effort in relatively modest ways by increasing local job creation, particularly in the agriculture sector, and to focus on social welfare and livelihoods. Meanwhile, anti-corruption investigations continue against former government officials, including Nawaz Sharif.

The Maldives

In 2014, President Xi used his visit to the Maldives – the first ever visit by a Chinese leader – as a means of rolling out substantial investment in the small archipelago state. Abdulla Yameen, who served as President of the Maldives from 2013 to 2018, welcomed China's role. As in other cases, Beijing utilized government-level agreements to avoid competitive procedures and secure project rights, and leveraged financial commitments conditioned on the use of Chinese firms to ensure their engagement.

Xi's visit in 2014 yielded visible results, including a 2-kilometer bridge connecting the Maldivian capital, Male, to an artificial island where the country's international airport is located along with room for expansion. And yet these results did not translate into political strength for the Yameen regime, which lost power following elections in September 2018.

The mechanics of China's behaviour in the Maldives drew backlash. In the run-up to the September 2018 general elections, Yameen's government was hammered by criticism of the terms of the agreements with China. The bridge project, for example, had been estimated by the government to cost slightly over $100 million, while Yameen accepted a $300 million loan for the project. The eventual victor and current President, Ibrahim Solih, alleged official corruption and self-dealing on the part of Yameen. Former President Mohamed Nasheed levied the nationalistic allegation that Yameen's mismanagement of the country's debt profile meant that China might be able to demand effective cessation of Maldivian territory if payments were not timely.[21]

The Maldives' small size and isolated position have the dual effect of making it dependent on foreign financing for large investments, including key climate resiliency activities, while also not being dependent on a single country for trade, electricity or other requirements. China accounted for 20 per cent of Maldivian imports in 2017, largely in goods and commodities essential for construction. China's exports to the Maldives more than doubled since before President Xi's 2014 visit, while Maldivian exports to China remained negligible.[22] But it is too early to tell whether President Solih's government will be able to renegotiate the terms of deals with China it inherited.

Conclusion

This study shows that in Nepal, Malaysia, Pakistan, and The Maldives – the four BRI recipient states in South or Southeast Asia that experienced a change in government after competitive electoral processes in the last two years – the new government expressed frustration with the terms of the BRI and sought to renegotiate, adjust, or otherwise modify those terms with China.

At a certain level this is not surprising – flawed democracies make fickle partners. In the literature, five factors are commonly identified as the sources of weakness among flawed democracies: "short-termism," or the difficulty democracies tend to have in managing long-term problems due to electoral cycles; "pain aversion," or the tendency of democratically elected leaders to put off near-term pain due to electoral interests; "elite capture," or the weakness of systems that allow elected senior-leaders to be influenced by financial gain, either for electoral or corrupt purposes; "division and conflict," or the centrifugal effects on societal cohesion of contested elections; and "voter ignorance," or the unpredictable and sometimes irrational choices made by voters who form the bedrock of a democracy.[23]

These common tenets make flawed democracies vulnerable to outside influence – including from China – also mean that outside influence is often fragile and temporary. Democratic transitions represent an opportunity to correct past mistakes, when responsibly managed. Several flaws in the design of China's BRI stand out across cases.

First, the most popular grievance toward China's investment is corruption. But in each case, corruption concerns were directed inward toward responsible officials, not toward the Chinese firms involved. Flawed democracies were institutionally porous enough to open substantial opportunities for corruption, without being capable enough to seek remediation across borders. Democratic transitions helped to reveal corruption and focus attention against it – even while struggling to address the underlying structural problems.

Second, the scale of CPEC financial obligations is a recurring concern. Nepal, Pakistan, and the Maldives are each far more debt stressed than Malaysia, but in each case direct and indirect repayment and tariff obligations caused controversy. Financial obligations made for short-term political benefit were quickly challenged even in flawed democracies, once those expedient benefits were exhausted through a political transition.

Third, the demand for local participation grew as the activities of Chinese firms became more visible. In each of the three cases, local business groups have voiced loud concern about being crowded out by Chinese firms. But little has been done to resolve this issue; the new governments in each case were challenged to find meaningful ways to alter the terms of China's engagement. In The Maldives, the smallest of the economies examined, the scale of Chinese debt obligations has led to fears that a future government could be vulnerable to greater concessions to Chinese control, including over territorial management rights as occurred with the Hambantota port in Sri Lanka, should the country default on debt payments.

Outside influence from third countries was typically not a primary driver of local assertiveness toward BRI projects. Nepal was the sole case where an external actor allegedly had a strong role in spurring concern. In no case was a third country's offer of assistance, including financial support, a motivation.

In 2019, three flawed democracies or hybrid regimes in South or Southeast Asia who are recipients of Chinese investment have elections scheduled to potentially replace executive leadership: the Philippines, Thailand, and Sri Lanka. If these elections produce a change in leadership, it is likely that new leadership will seek a better deal with China, among other states. This persistent drum beat of assertiveness on the part of local regimes will continue so long as China's flawed business model remains unchanged.

NOTES

1. https://www.fbicgroup.com/sites/default/files/B&R_Initiative_65_Countries_and_Beyond.pdf (accessed 14 March 2019).
2. https://foreignpolicy.com/2018/05/16/on-chinas-new-silk-road-democracy-pays-a-toll/ (accessed 14 March 2019).
3. https://www.foreignaffairs.com/articles/china/2018-10-24/why-democracies-are-turning-against-belt-and-road (accessed 14 March 2019).
4. Mongolia, Indonesia, Malaysia, Philippines, Singapore, Timor-Leste, Israel, Lebanon, Palestine, Afghanistan, India, Sri Lanka, Albania, Armenia, Bulgaria, Croatia, Czech Republic, Estonia, Hungary, Latvia, Lithuania, Poland, Romania, Serbia, Slovakia, and Slovenia.
5. Thailand, Kyrgyzstan, Iraq, Bangladesh, Bhutan, Maldives, Nepal, Pakistan, Bosnia and Herzegovina, Georgia, Macedonia, Moldova, Montenegro, Turkey, and Ukraine.
6. https://www.economist.com/graphic-detail/2019/01/08/the-retreat-of-global-democracy-stopped-in-2018 (accessed 14 March 2019).
7. Italy's March 2019 announcement that it would sign a memorandum of understanding with China in which it signs up to the Belt & Road Initiative does not change this finding, as Italy is also identified as a "flawed democracy" in the 2018 index.
8. China, Brunei, Cambodia, Laos, Myanmar, Vietnam, Kazakhstan, Tajikistan, Turkmenistan , Uzbekistan, Bahrain, Egypt, Iran, Jordan, Kuwait, Oman, Qatar, Saudi Arabia, Syria, UAE, Yemen, Azerbaijan, Belarus, and Russia.
9. Amara Thiha, 'Myanmar Speeds up Progress on China's Belt and Road'. https://thediplomat.com/2018/12/myanmar-speeds-up-progress-on-chinas-belt-and-road/ (accessed 14 March 2019).
10. We excluded Bangladesh because its leadership did not change as a result of its 2018 election. While Bangladesh is characterized as a hybrid system by the EIU in 2018, its standing may further erode given the allegations of widespread irregularities that plagued the election, which returned Prime Minister Sheikh Hasina and her party to power with an overwhelming majority.
11. https://asia.nikkei.com/Politics/International-relations/Nepal-hitches-railway-to-Chinese-standards-in-blow-to-India (accessed 14 March 2019).
12. https://thediplomat.com/2018/06/nepal-china-reality-sets-in/ (accessed 14 March 2019).
13. Data from MIT OEC, accessible at http://atlas.media.mit.edu/g0uv3c (accessed 14 March 2019).
14. https://www.scmp.com/week-asia/geopolitics/article/2161968/nepals-west-seti-hydropower-project-jeopardy-china-eyes-exit (accessed 14 March 2019).
15. https://www.scmp.com/week-asia/politics/article/2161805/what-malaysias-mahathir-really-plans-china-backed-projects-cant (accessed 14 March 2019).
16. https://www.scmp.com/week-asia/politics/article/2166693/chinas-belt-and-road-colonialism-mahathir-not-all (accessed 14 March 2019).
17. https://atlas.media.mit.edu/en/profile/country/mys/ (accessed 14 March 2019).

18. https://thediplomat.com/2019/03/is-new-malaysias-china-us-balance-changing-under-mahathir/ (accessed 14 March 2019).
19. https://www.ft.com/content/d4a3e7f8-b282-11e8-99ca-68cf89602132 (accessed 14 March 2019).
20. https://tribune.com.pk/story/1815954/2-govt-cuts-cpec-rail-project-2-billion/ (accessed 14 March 2019).
21. https://www.ft.com/content/c8da1c8a-2a19-11e9-88a4-c32129756dd8 (accessed 14 March 2019).
22. Data accessed via MIT OEC. https://atlas.media.mit.edu/en/profile/country/mdv/ (accessed 14 March 2019).
23. Thomas Carothers, 'Is Democracy The Problem?'. *National Interest*, January 16, 2019, https://carnegieendowment.org/2019/01/16/is-democracy-problem-pub-78137 (accessed 14 March 2019).

IS THE BELT AND ROAD INITIATIVE A CHINESE GEO-POLITICAL STRATEGY?

YIWEI WANG AND XUEJUN LIU

Introduction

This article starts from the premise that today's world is growing ever more chaotic. Poverty and the wealth gap are the most devastating sources of this chaos. As the old saying goes, "thieves are the children of poverty". Poverty in a country is a potential source of international chaos, and the wealth gap has helped to trigger and worsen the chaos. A report released on January 18 2016 by Oxfam, an institution for poverty relief and development, shows that the wealth of the world's 62 richest people is equal to that of the world's poorest people, who account for half the total population of humankind. Moreover, the wealth of the richest 1% is more than that of the remaining 99% combined.[1] The world's wealth gap has been increasingly widened, and the rich are getting richer at an ever faster rate.[2] In this context, turmoil is no longer exclusive to less developed countries; it has been born in or spread to developed ones, as manifest in refugee crises, terrorist attacks, and the rise in extremism.

All these are closely related to the fate of the Silk Road countries.

The two great civilizations of the East and the West were linked by the Silk Road earlier in history. After its rise in the 15th century, the

Turkish Ottoman Empire (the so-called "Wall of Ottoman") straitened trade along the centuries-old ancient Silk Road. After that, the Europeans were forced to go to sea, and ushered in the era of globalization through colonization. The Silk Road declined. The Eastern civilization became closed and conservative. And the modern world entered an era of Western-centrism.

For millennia, Europeans got oriental spices, porcelain, tea and many other goods through the Silk Road. China's "four great inventions" also spread to Europe through the Arab world, which became one of the factors triggering the European Renaissance. The fall of the Silk Road also influenced Europe in a profound way, being one of the factors which led to the discovery and conquest of the New World of the Americas.

The Euro-centric world is inextricably linked with the rise of ocean-borne transport to function as the major carrier of globalization. 71% of the Earth's surface is covered by oceans, and 90% of trade is conducted by sea. To this day, according to World Bank statistics, 80% of the world's total output comes from areas within 100 km from the coast lines. This is, arguably, the story of the modern world: the marginalized countries rose and the central areas of civilization collapsed. From Portugal to Spain, and to the Netherlands, Britain and the United States, great powers rose because of their proximity to the ocean and its opportunities for easy trade and transport, while older land-based civilizations declined. Even until the end of the 1980s, the rhetoric of the "death of rivers" (declining "yellow" civilizations developed around rivers and great land-masses as compared to thriving "blue" civilizations relying on seas) were still popular in China.[3]

Since then, the world again fell into a period of "stability-turmoil," and geopolitics and power games went rampant. The "world system" and the "dependency theory" have revealed the root causes why marginalized countries in the map of globalization cannot shake off backwardness and unrest. Under these viewpoints, richer countries have benefitted from a flow of resources which have come from poorer nations, and the "world system" has entrenched this situation.

"The end of any development usually gives rise to changes, changes open ways for development, continuous development can of course last long." How to solve the worldwide problem of poverty and how to narrow the wealth gap? How to evolve from "change" to "continuous development"? Historical experience tells us that to free ourselves from the world's periodic "stability-turmoil" law, it is necessary to restore the diversity of the world, balance the relationships between land and ocean, East and West, and South and North, and achieve the connectivity of the world.

Since the decline of the ancient Silk Road, the revival of the road has become a common dream of countries along the old routes, not to mention the idea of the Eurasian continent again becoming the center of human civilization through its redeveloped connectivity. The United Nations Development Program (UNDP) is a pioneer in this field, with its proposal to connect the maritime transport lines at the two ends of the Eurasian continent with a railway. This is known as the Eurasian Land Bridge Plan.

However, the historical responsibility for making these dreams a reality falls on the shoulders of 21st-century China.

Since ancient times, the Eurasian continent has been the central stage of world politics; the destiny of Eurasia reflected the destiny of humankind. Mindful of this, the British geo-political scientist Halford Mackinder called the Eurasian continent the "World Island", with his ideas that "Who rules East Europe commands the Heartland; Who rules the Heartland commands the World Island; Who rules the World Island commands the World."[4]

Mackinder argued that "The revolution commenced by the great mariners of the Columbian generation endowed Christendom with the widest possible mobility of power … The broad political effect was to reverse the relations of Europe and Asia."[5]

Indeed, before the great discoveries of the 15th and 16th centuries, the center of the world was the Eurasian continent, a continent extending from the Spanish coasts to the coasts of China. The main trade route back then was the Silk Road. And, Europe, Great Britain in particular, was obviously at the rim of the world. In 1453, the Ottoman Empire occupied Constantinople, breaking the Silk Road that once linked East and West. In order to find a new route towards Oriental wealth, people started the endeavor that finally led to geographical discovery. Geographical discoveries ushered in the era of sea-power, because one simple geographical fact is that the interconnected oceans formed a whole. It was the oceans that proved the global value of sea-power in modern times. At the same time, geographical discovery ushered in the era of Western-centered globalization. The West was no longer at the rim far from the heartland, but the center of the world. In the past 500 years, Europe dominated the globalization process during the first 400 years, and later the US. This is the political core of globalization. However, "Entering the 21st century, it is clear that the American-style globalization system is tending to collapse. And China is not only the biggest winner of globalization in the past 30 years, but is also becoming the main leader of globalization in the 21st century. The gyroscope of the global system is turning to China."[6]

A watershed in the history of humanity is approaching. According to Mckinsey's projection of global economic center of gravity, "after a millennium, world economic center is returning to the East."

This model indicates that, after the Song Dynasty (960–1279), the world economic center of gravity shifted from China to Europe, and later to the United States, and will shift back to China in 2025, which can be called a return of the original world. The most rapid shift in the world's economic center of gravity happened in 2000–2010, a period we just experienced. During 2000–2025, humans will have made a step as big as the past century (1820–1913).

The economic base determines the superstructure. The world's economic center of gravity is shifting eastward, so is the political center. With the Western-centered world fading away, the diversity of the world is coming back.

With a view to promote global rebalancing, China has proposed the Belt and Road Initiative, which is in line with the law governing the evolution of human civilization as well as the long cycle of world business. This Initiative has clarified the direction and brought hope for the elimination of the "stability-turmoil" cycle and the realization of common development.

Through further opening China's western doors to drive the development of western China as well as inland countries such as the Central Asian states and Mongolia, the Initiative strives to promote the idea of inclusive development, an important value of globalization. It has changed the old image of Central Asia and other Silk Road regions as being a development "lowland," merely passageways for east–west trade and cultural exchanges. Rather, it has enriched the value of the Eurasian Land Bridge with the concept of connectivity, and extended its reach to Africa and beyond, transcending past achievements in space and time.

The Belt and Road Initiative was part of the logic of China's reform and opening-up process. Originally, this change and opening-up was focused on southeast coastal areas and principally towards to the US. Nowadays, however, paying attention to the Eurasian continent, China has moved westward to embrace both the hinterland and oceans. More importantly, the Belt and Road Initiative aims to reverse the unjust, unsustainable trend of globalization.

After the miracle of reform and opening-up during the past 40 years created by the Chinese people under the leadership of the Communist Party of China, the remarkable achievements have benefitted China and beyond. "The Silk Road changed history, largely because the people who managed to traverse part or all of the Silk Road planted their cultures like seeds of exotic species carried to distant lands."[7] Aimed at reviving the Silk Road, the Belt and Road Initiative can be called the new Long March. It is China's declaration, ambassador and planter, expanding and deepening cooperation and friendship between China and the countries concerned. This Initiative will enhance China's prestige by largely improving the capability and credibility of "Made in China", "Created by China" and "Planned by China". In terms of its geo-economic and strategic effects, the Initiative can well be called the "second great geographical discovery." Reshaping the history of human civilization and the discourse power of globalization, the Initiative has reflected China's sense of global responsibility.

Is BRI a geo-political strategy?

China has harvested significant experience during the periods of Reform and Opening Up, particularly in the fields of problem solving and focusing on the realization of goals. The Belt and Road Initiative aims, in its essence, to build five metaphorical roads to fight gradually against three deficits. The five roads are a road towards peace, a road towards prosperity, a road towards opening up, a road to innovation and a road interlinking different civilizations. These, it is hoped will work to eliminate the deficits in peace, development, and governance.[8] A Community with a Shared Future is the original aspiration for both Chinese Communists and broader Chinese civilization, following the teachings of Confucius that all people under heaven are of one family and all nations should live in harmony.

Thus, Chinese President Xi Jinping said that the aim of putting forward the Belt and Road Initiative is to practice the concept of the "Community of Shared Future". In other words, the Belt and Road Initiative and the

Community of Shared Future are two sides of a coin which is also a manifestation of *He-he* (和合), or namely Chinese Harmonious and Syncretic Culture in a new era:

He—Harmony—The Community of Shared Future (the goal to be realised);
he—Syncretism—The Belt and Road Initiative (means of solving the problem).

Chinese *He-he* culture goes beyond the Western "divide and rule" culture. It is not a geo-political strategy, rather a "geo-economy" or "geo-civilization".

In the book *Connectography: Mapping the Future of Global Civilization*, the author Parag Khanna points out that the world is now evolving from a dependence on natural geography and political geography to functional geography.[9] The hardcore of the Belt and Road Initiative is connectivity, which brings together the destiny of the whole world aiming to embrace an ever-lasting peace, universal security, and a common prosperity, which is open and inclusive, and also environmentally conscious.[10] The Belt and Road Initiative is, on this account, not China's geopolitical strategy. On the contrary, it emphasizes strategic links and connectivity, with the aim of eliminating geopolitical barriers and the suffering caused by colonialism, and ultimately strengthening people-to-people ties.

Three Kingdoms, one of the four great classical novels of Chinese literature, begins with the saying "This world will separate after a long time united. Also it will do the opposite after a long time splitting". Unification, rather than division, is in the DNA of Chinese culture. The world in the present era has suffered much division: populism, nationalism, terrorism and so forth. What people now desire is peace and harmony, cooperation and prosperity.

Where does the misperception about the BRI come from?

The idea that the BRI is a geo-political strategy, comparing it to a New Silk Road version of the Marshall Plan, is not the only misperception about BRI. There are other intentional misperceptions about the Initiative on top of this. It is necessary to ask why has the Belt and Road Initiative been misunderstood on purpose?

First of all, it originates from a misunderstanding of China which arises in at least three ways. The first comes from the perceptions a number of foreign nations have of China. China's intentions, it should be said, are always questioned. Many outside China suppose that China is on the path of their past. Some, at the more extreme level, are fundamentally opposed to any initiative taken by China, even if it is a reasonable policy. These approaches to China are epitomized in the misunderstanding of the Belt and Road Initiative.

The second one comes from a misunderstanding of the times: people are always accustomed to looking at new-born things from a historical perspective, regarding the Belt and Road as a simple revival of the ancient silk roads. In addition, the view of history is also a kind of selective memory which is based on its own historical experience but not China or the world itself. The Belt and Road Initiative is an idea viewing the world from the day after tomorrow, rather than from yesterday. What this initiative desires to achieve is to rejuvenate the spirit of the ancient Silk Roads, that is peace and cooperation, openness and inclusiveness, mutual learning and benefit and eventually to build a community with a shared future.

Thirdly, the misunderstanding of BRI stems from self-righteousness. Consideration of others is an acceptable virtue in Chinese tradition; however, it is not uncommon to measure the stature of great men by the yardstick of small men. Some people argue that the Belt and Road Initiative is a Chinese Marshall Plan according to the unconscious logic of western powers, or indeed argue that it constitutes "strategic overstretch" on the part of China. What they truly believe is that superpowers must intend, by their very nature, to take over the whole world. Yet, the Belt and Road Initiative itself is not a strategy on how China should attain such a position. Some scholars hold the view that BRI is a "strategic overstretch".[11] The Belt and Road Initiative, it should be said, bring "three outlooks" into play: a China outlook, the world outlook (based on the new era) and the western outlook (based on its own).

Karl Marx began to learn English at the age of sixty and lived in the United Kingdom in his later years. He suggested that when using a foreign language, people should try to forget all about their own native languages. Today, people always take the familiar western-centric background as the frame of reference, so that the Belt and Road Initiative becomes a "New Silk Road Strategy" and China is regarded as attempting to behave in the fashion in which western powers have done in the past. That is the major reason why they misconceive the Belt and Road Initiative as a Chinese geopolitical strategy.

Such a misunderstanding is not, however, the greatest matter for concern. The most terrible thing is to be confused but to pretend to know everything. As one saying goes, "You can't wake a person who is pretending to be asleep". In fact, even if we in China make all efforts, it may be unlikely to change some unfriendly international public opinions and the stereotypes of China and BRI accordingly. As a result, the only good option is to confront these concerns calmly and confidently, and do what we are able to do to fully prepare and be faced with these challenges.

NOTES

1. Larry Elliott, 'Richest 62 People as Wealthy as Half of World's Population, Says Oxfam'. *The Guardian*, January 18, 2016, https://www.theguardian.com/business/2016/jan/18/richest-62-billionaires-wealthy-half-world-population-combined (accessed 9 March 2019).
2. Winnie Byanyima, 'Our Struggles for a Better World Are All Threatened by the Inequality Crisis'. *Huffpost*, January 20, 2016, http://www.huffingtonpost.com/winnie-byanyima/our-struggles-for-a-bette_b_9026582.html (accessed 9 March 2019).
3. Wang Yiwei, *Death of Oceans?: Revelations of European Civilization*. Shanghai: Shanghai People's Publishing House, 2013.
4. H. J. Mackinder, *The Geographical Pivot of History*. Beijing: Commercial Press, 2015, p. 15.
5. H. J. Mackinder, *The Geographical Pivot of History*. Beijing: Commercial Press, 2015, pp. 64–65.
6. Bao Shenggang, 'The Second Geographical Discovery'. *United Morning Post*, May 5, 2015. Of course, despite the European conquest of the Americas and even South Asia, as late as the late 18th century, the Europeans had not yet established a dominant position over East Asia with China at the center and the Islamic world with the Ottoman Empire at the center, both on the major plate of Eurasia. Europe's worldwide advantage lasted at best only two hundred years, but is often said to be five hundred years. – Author's note.
7. Valerie Hansen, (Zhang Zhan trans.), *The Silk Road: A New History*. Beijing: Beijing United Publishing Company, 2015, p. 207.
8. Xi Jinping, 'Work Together to Build the Silk Road Economic Belt and the 21st Century Maritime Silk Road'. *Xinhua News*, May 14, 2017, http://www.xinhuanet.com/politics/2017-05/14/c_1120969677.htm (accessed 5 March 2019).
9. Parag Khanna, *Connectography: Mapping the Future of Global Civilization*. New York: Random House, 2016.
10. Xi Jinping, 'Work Together to Build a Community of Shared Future for Mankind'. *Xinhua News*, January 18, 2017, http://www.xinhuanet.com/world/2017-01/19/c_1120340081.htm (accessed 5 March 2019).
11. An idea developed according to the logic of Paul Kennedy, *The Rise and Fall of the Great Powers: Economic Change and Military Conflict From 1500 to 2000*. Random House, 1987.

CHINA-PAKISTAN ECONOMIC CORRIDOR – IS IT THE ROAD TO THE FUTURE?

NALANDA ROY

Introduction

> In all of history, except for the Marshall Plan, there was practically no long-term project which needs enormous courage. Let me express my gratitude for the People's Republic of China for this courage, and especially let me appreciate China's president for the courage which is so rare.[1]
>
> Milos Zeman, Czech President

Asia is the world's largest and most populous continent. It makes up 30 percent of the Earth's land area and houses approximately 60 percent (4.3 billion people) of the world's total population. Asia's rich cultural heritage and history continue to modernize along with its developing economies, and it is fast becoming one of the world's most dynamic economic regions. Currently, Asia is in the midst of a geopolitical transformation with vital developments taking place all across the continent. For example, the rise of China both economically and militarily; the rise of India; the power game between countries to increase commercial influence throughout Eurasia and beyond; and the continued presence of the United States to address this power dynamic are all signs that show that Asia is fast becoming a "flashpoint" in the global platform. Some of the world's most important sea lanes, roughly two-thirds of the world's oil, and a third of the world's bulk cargo go through the Strait of Malacca,[2] thereby making this region a significant player in the global geostrategic orbit.

Napoleon Bonaparte once made a comment about China, stating that we should, "let her sleep, for when she wakes, she will shake the world." Years later, this statement rings true. Geostrategic dominance is now being driven by Beijing. China's capital has become increasingly brazen in its attempts to enforce its claims in Asia's troubled waters. As Beijing's role in the international system grows more prominent, Chinese foreign policy can be readily described as a "moving target" with their country heavily integrated in all parts of this new system. In this regard, one of the major initiatives taken by China is the development of the 'New Silk Road' or the Belt and Road Initiative (BRI)/One Belt One Road (OBOR) initiatives. It is believed that this umbrella initiative has the potential to yield economic and political gains for Beijing and the BRI countries.

This paper will analyze the security and economic implications of the BRI-linked corridor projects, particularly the China-Pakistan Economic Corridor (CPEC) project; examine the security and economic implications of the project; explain whether Pakistan's burgeoning relationship with China is a matter of concern for her neighbours; and finally consider the future prospects for the CPEC.

OBOR – background of the initiative

> As I stand here and look back at that episode of history, I could almost hear the camel bells echoing in the mountains and see the wisp of smoke rising from the desert.
>
> Xi Jinping

In 2013, Chinese President Xi Jinping proposed the joint construction of the Silk Road Economic Belt and the 21st-Century Maritime Silk Road to reconnect the world, promote world peace, and offer a new direction to the global economy. At the China-ASEAN Expo in 2013, Chinese Premier Li Keqiang emphasized the need to build the Maritime Silk Road with an ASEAN orientation to help promote the economic prosperity of the Belt and Road Initiative (BRI) countries. Figure 1 shows the One Belt One Road (OBOR) plan based around two core conduits: the Silk Road Economic Belt and the twenty-first Century Maritime Silk Road.

The Belt and Road Initiative (BRI) is an ambitious effort to improve regional cooperation and connectivity on a transcontinental scale. The goal is to connect Asia, Europe, and Africa along five routes. This is a flagship project that aims to transform the economic environment in the region and enhance regional cooperation. The Silk Road Economic

Figure 1 The overland and maritime routes of the One Belt One Road Initiative. Source: Council on Foreign Relations.

Belt focuses on: (1) linking China to Europe through Central Asia and Russia; (2) connecting China with the Middle East through Central Asia; and (3) bringing together China and Southeast Asia, South Asia and the Indian Ocean. The twenty-first Century Maritime Silk Road focuses on using Chinese coastal ports to (4) link China with Europe through the South China Sea and the Indian Ocean, and (5) connect China with the South Pacific Ocean through the South China Sea. The initiative aims to strengthen infrastructure, trade, and investment ties between China and some 65 other countries that account collectively for over 30 percent of global GDP, 62 percent of the population, and 75 percent of known energy reserves.

According to the Chinese Academy of International Trade and Economic Cooperation (MOFCO), the objective of the One Belt One Road initiative is to realize the "China Dream," which was the slogan advocated by Xi Jinping.[3] Beijing predicts that China's annual trade with BRI countries will surpass $2.5 trillion by 2025,[4] growing more rapidly than its trade with the rest of the world. Even smaller economies like Pakistan and Bangladesh will receive a big boost. Table 1 shows the year and name changes associated with the Silk Road initiatives.

Table 1 Source: Created by the author.

Year	Silk Road Projects introduced by the PRC
2013	Economic Belt along the Silk Road and shortly afterward the twenty-first century Maritime Silk Road
2014	One Belt One Road (OBOR)
2017	Belt and Road Initiative (BRI)
2018	Trans-Pacific Maritime Silk Road and the Polar Silk Road

Key areas of OBOR cooperation

Focusing on the above five routes, the BRI will take advantage of international transport routes, core cities, and key ports to further strengthen collaboration and build six international economic cooperation corridors. These have been identified as the New Eurasia Land Bridge, China-Mongolia-Russia, China-Central Asia-West Asia, China-Indochina Peninsula, China-Pakistan, and Bangladesh-China-India-Myanmar. Figure 2 shows the six corridors involved in the BRI project.

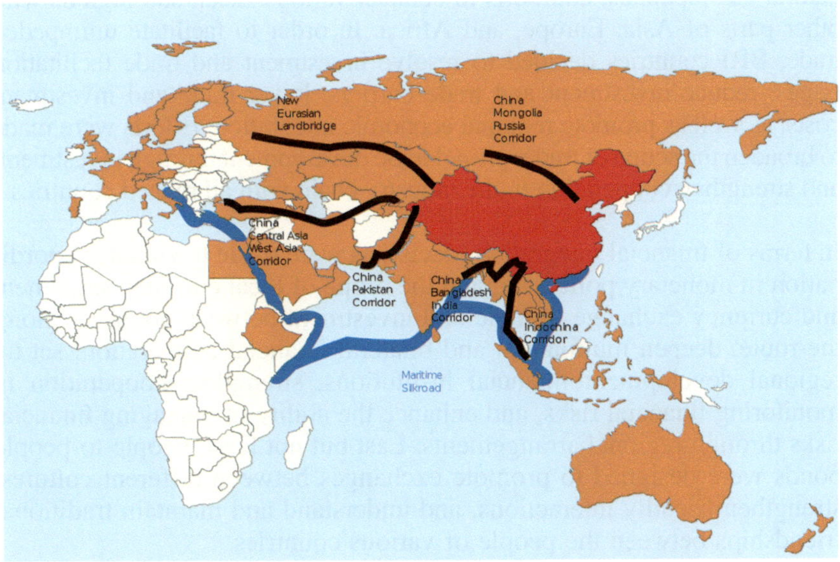

Figure 2 The Six Economic Corridors of the BRI. Source: https://upload.wikimedia.org/wikipedia/commons/thumb/c/cb/One-belt-one-road.svg/1280px-One-belt-one-road.svg.png.

The BRI is in line with the purposes and principles of the UN Charter and upholds the Five Principles of Peaceful Coexistence. They have mutual respect for each other's sovereignty and territorial integrity, mutual non-aggression, mutual non-interference in internal affairs, mutual benefit and equality, and peaceful coexistence. The initiative was declared to be harmonious and inclusive, and therefore open to all countries. At the outset, it was also decided that the BRI would abide by international market rules and norms in order to benefit everyone.[5] Five major goals of the BRI formed the basis for the advancement of regional cooperation. The goals are policy coordination, facilities connectivity, unimpeded trade, financial integration, and people-to-people bonds.

In terms of policy coordination, countries along the Belt and Road will jointly formulate development plans and measures for advancing cross-national and regional cooperation, resolve problems arising from cooperation through consultation, and jointly provide policy support to practical cooperation and large-scale project implementation. In terms of facilities connectivity, the idea was to prioritize areas of construction. Initiatives were made to remove barriers and bottleneck areas of core international transportation passages. The connectivity of infrastructure facilities included the promotion of railways, highways, air routes, telecommunications, oil and natural gas pipelines, and ports to connect various Asian sub-regions with other parts of Asia, Europe, and Africa. In order to facilitate unimpeded trade, BRI countries decided to resolve investment and trade facilitation issues, reduce investment and trade barriers, lower trade and investment costs, as well as promote regional economic integration. Efforts were made to broaden the scope of trade, propel trade development through investment, and strengthen cooperation in the industry chain with all related countries.

In terms of financial integration, decisions were made to enhance coordination in monetary policy, expand the scope of local currency settlement and currency exchange in trade and investment between countries along the route, deepen multilateral and bilateral financial cooperation, set up regional development financial institutions, strengthen cooperation in monitoring financial risks, and enhance the ability of managing financial risks through regional arrangements. Last but not least, people-to-people bonds were designed to promote exchanges between different cultures, strengthen friendly interactions, and understand and maintain traditional friendships between the people of various countries.

In December 2014, China proposed the $40 billion (USD) Silk Road Fund that would finance the *Belt and Road Initiative*. It was decided that the Fund would comply with international market rules and finance, and would solicit active participation from investors like the China-Africa Development Fund, and Asian Infrastructure Investment Bank. On 14 May 2017, President Xi Jinping at the opening ceremony of the "Belt and Road Forum for International Cooperation" announced that China would contribute an additional 100 billion yuan ($15 billion) to the Silk Road Fund. However, over the past couple of years, BRI-linked corridor projects – like the China-Pakistan Economic Corridor (CPEC) in Pakistan – have emerged as a major source of tension in Asian geopolitics.

CPEC – the road to the future?

> CPEC is an epoch-making project going to put Pakistan-China friendship and their economic cooperation to new heights.
>
> Shehbaz Sharif

The concept of the China-Pakistan Economic Corridor was first discussed by Premier Li Keqiang during his visit to Pakistan in May 2013. At the time, the objective was to build an economic corridor running from Kashgar, Xinjiang in the north to Pakistan's Gwadar Port in the south. At present, the two governments have mapped out a provisional long-term plan for building highways, railways, oil and natural gas pipelines and, optic-fibre networks stretching from Kashgar to Gwadar Port. The significance of both the Karachi and Gwadar port facilities can't be underestimated. They serve as major trans-shipment points for China's energy and resource needs. They also give China direct access to the Persian Gulf and the Horn of Africa – including its naval base in Djibouti – via the Arabian Sea and the Indian Ocean.[6] According to a joint declaration issued by China and Pakistan in Islamabad in April 2015, the two countries will proactively advance key cooperation projects, including Phase II of the upgrade and renovation of the Karakoram Highway (the Thakot-Havelian section), an expressway at the east bay of Gwadar Port, a new international airport, an expressway from Karachi to Lahore (the Multan-Sukkur section), the Lahore rail transport orange line, the Haier-Ruba economic zone, and the China-Pakistan cross-national optic fibre network.[7] There might be a possibility that CPEC could have a useful "demonstration effect, indicating to other investors that Pakistan is a safe and attractive destination for foreign direct investment."[8] Figure 3 shows the proposed corridor.

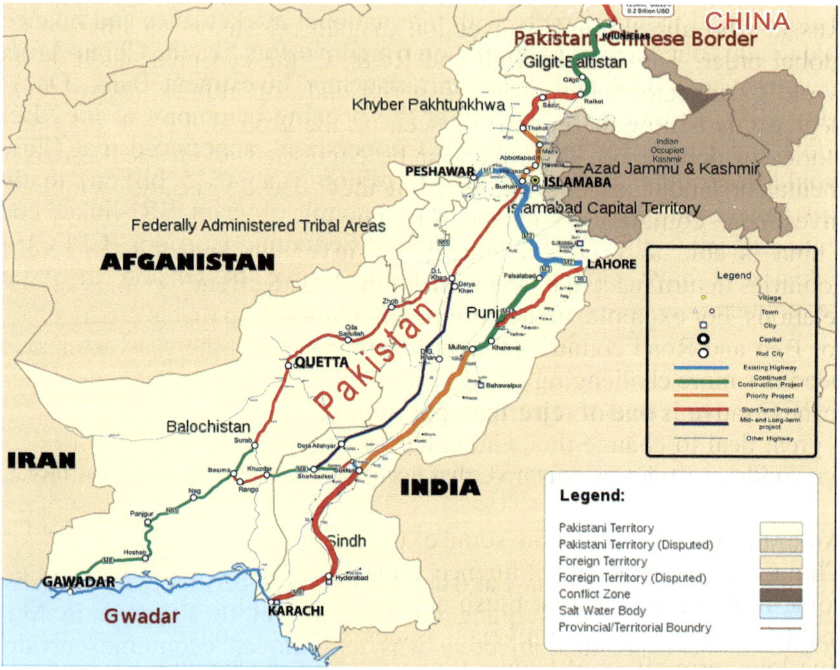

Figure 3 The Proposed China-Pakistan Economic Corridor (CPEC). Source: https://upload.wikimedia.org/wikipedia/commons/8/88/China_Pakistan_Economic_Corridor.jpg.

The CPEC deal grants the Chinese 40-years of operation rights to the port, which is hugely significant for Beijing because it will allow:

a. China to ship some of its oil from the Persian Gulf to the port and pump it through the pipelines to western China.
b. China will be able to save billions in transportation costs, as well as time.
c. Pakistan – Gwadar, in particular – will play a critical role in China's joint plans for a Silk Road Economic Belt and a Maritime Silk Road linking China to Europe and beyond.

A Long-Term Plan for CPEC (2017-2030) was released in December 2017. The report defines the project broadly as "a growth axis and a development belt", with "the comprehensive transportation corridor and industrial cooperation between Pakistan and China as the main axis" and "concrete economic and trade cooperation" as "the engine."[9] The CPEC timeline stated that the short-term projects would be completed by 2020; medium-term projects should be close to completion by 2025; and long-term projects should be in place by 2030. As China integrates more with the global economy, it was expected that Beijing would further open its economy and strengthen its mutually beneficial cooperation with countries in Asia, Europe, and Africa. Therefore, China is committed to shouldering more duties and obligations for the benefit of mankind.

The China-Pakistan energy corridor would be an expensive proposition for Beijing given the long distances, rugged terrain, transnational threats, and insurgency movements involved. Gwadar's Baluchistan province is also prone to separatist violence. At the geopolitical level, however, the proposal is attractive because of Gwadar's proximity to the Persian Gulf. All maritime choke points, save for the Strait of Hormuz, would be effectively bypassed. Besides, Pakistan is a close ally of the PRC. Therefore, the Chinese leadership seems to be taking the proposal seriously. Plans for the CPEC were formalized in 2015 when Pakistan and China signed fifty-one agreements and memoranda of understanding on the $46 billion Chinese investment. While outlining the importance of Pakistan in the BRI policy, Chinese Foreign Minister Wang Yi commented:

> "If One Belt, One Road is like a symphony involving and benefiting every country, then the construction of the China-Pakistan Economic Corridor is the sweet melody of the symphony's first movement."[10]

Pakistan has the potential to serve as a nexus for the Silk Road Economic Belt and the Maritime Silk Road. Over time, an overland link across Pakistan to the Arabian Sea would help alleviate China's heavy dependence on the Malacca and Lombok/Makassar straits in Southeast Asia. This is a serious concern for China because the Malacca Strait is a very narrow and congested waterway. But the strait is considered vital because it is the shortest route between the Indian and Pacific oceans. More than 60,000 vessels transit the strait each year, carrying 25 percent of global trade. In fact, 85 percent of China's oil imports travel through the single chokepoint of the Strait of Malacca.[11] Hence, the strait has both geopolitical and geostrategic significance for China, and the leaders have given considerable attention to the "Malacca dilemma."[12]

> Peace and development go hand in hand. 'One Belt, One Road' signifies that geo-economics must take precedence over geopolitics and that the center of gravity should shift from conflict to cooperation. We see it as a path for overcoming terrorism and extremism.[13]
>
> Nawaz Sharif

Now the question stands whether the CPEC is an international extension of China's effort to deliver security through economic development? If the massive investment package ($46 billion deal) between China and Pakistan gets implemented over the next 15 years, it will not only pull Pakistan into China's geostrategic orbit but will also be a game-changer for the region. This deal is essentially a package of major projects that fall into two domains: transportation and energy. The former involves a rail link connecting Gwadar; a deep-sea commercial port on Pakistan's southern coast to the western Chinese city of Kashgar; building a 125-mile tunnel linking the two countries; upgrading a number of existing highways (including the critical Karachi-Lahore section). The latter includes building pipelines to transport oil and gas to Kashgar; the completion of the Iran-Pakistan gas pipeline; various coal, wind, solar, and hydro energy plants that would add some 10,000 megawatts to energy-starved Pakistan by 2019. Kashgar is an oasis city in China's Xinjiang region that dates back more than 2000 years. The city serves as a key trading post along the historical Silk Road. More recently, Kashgar has been plagued by violent attacks, which Beijing blames on separatists and terrorists. The local government has stepped up police patrols and offered financial rewards for tip-offs about violent attacks, but very little has been accomplished.

Gwadar – a jewel in the crown?

> Our friends are happy with the CPEC project, while the enemy is quite unnerved due to this gigantic project.
>
> Shehbaz Sharif

The Gwadar Port in Baluchistan province has become a major point of contention between China and India. Gwadar is a warm-water, deep-sea port, which is located 400 km away from the Straits of Hormuz. This port has become a critical choke point in the Persian Gulf. Besides, 80 percent of China's imports pass through the Straits of Malacca. The Port is also located on the shores of the Arabian Sea about 533 km from Karachi and 120 km from the Iranian border. Whenever tensions flare up, both of these straits become extremely vulnerable. The Gwadar port development project commenced in 2002 with huge investments by both Chinese and Pakistani investors. The main idea was to transform Gwadar into a dominant port that would benefit the locals. In fact, with the CPEC project and Gwadar, China will be at the doorstep of Hormuz. China realized that such an arrangement could eventually eliminate the Malacca dilemma. Additionally, it is the main feature of the China-Pakistan Economic Corridor, and the key to the belt and road initiative because the port is at the heart of the $50 billion Chinese investment in the CPEC. It is the jewel in the crown for China! Hence, it is essential for Beijing to develop Gwadar, so that they would have a firm and reliable long-term beachhead in not only the Indian Ocean but also the Persian Gulf, thereby, effectively making it a *two-ocean power*.

Pakistan awarded the contract for construction and operation to China in 2013. China Overseas Port Holding Company plans to expand Gwadar Port by constructing nine new multipurpose berths along 3.2 km of seafront to the east of the existing berths. The shipping route from the Middle East to China via the strait is about 12,000 km long. Gwadar port will even provide alternative shipping routes to the Malacca Strait. The Port is considered a crucial link between the land-based belt and the maritime road. Pakistani Prime Minister Nawaz Sharif said that over four generations, ties with China had "remained robust" despite both internal political changes and major regional developments. He further reiterated the notion that, "our relations are based on the shared ideals and principles of mutual trust, mutual benefit, and mutual respect."[14] Thus, the investment will help strengthen Pakistan's struggling economy and also lessen its dependence on its few existing and overwhelmed ports. The CPEC will also enhance Pakistan's power generation capacity, and reduce unemployment and poverty. However, there are serious security concerns for China about violence from ethnic Uighurs in its predominantly Muslim north-western Xinjiang region. The separatist insurgency in Baluchistan province, where the economic corridor starts, also makes that region extremely volatile.[15] Moreover, the Baluch people (3 percent of its population) fear that their resources are being exploited by outsiders and that they will soon be turned into a minority group.

India is upset with the China-Pakistan Economic Corridor because it runs through the disputed Gilgit-Baltistan region, part of the erstwhile state of Jammu and Kashmir, which is contested by both India and Pakistan. India is also worried that the Pakistan-China pipeline that runs parallel to the Karakorum highway running from Gwadar to Kashgar in Xinjiang could turn out to be a hub for the PLA Navy.[16] The most difficult area to control are the borders in Kashmir, where Pakistan, India, and China all have competing claims and the line of control (LOC) remains the de-facto international frontier within Kashmir. Because of China's constant use of the veto power to throttle India's proposals at the

United Nations Security Council (UNSC), and the recent terrorist attack in Pulwama, India in which Pakistan based Jaish-e-Muhammed (JeM) had claimed responsibility for the terror attack, the situation has worsened.

Both Gwadar and the Iranian Chabahar port are competing to gain access in the Central Asian Region (CAR) markets. The Chabahar port is located in the south of Sistan and Baluchistan Province of Iran and is the only Iranian port with direct access to the Indian Ocean. It has historically been a trading centre because of its access to the Oman Sea and the Persian Gulf. The port will be connected to the Trans-Iranian railway with the completion of the Kerman-Zahedan railway. Thanks to the port of Chabahar, it's easy for India to trade with Central Asian Republics, Afghanistan, and Iran. India is also providing landlocked Afghanistan greater access to the Indian market; inaugurated an air freight corridor to boost bilateral trade.[17] Moreover, unlike Gwadar, Chabahar does not lie in a disturbing and insurgency-ridden area. Hence, strategic countries like India prefer Chabahar for easy trading and for dealing with security needs in the region. In fact, India is trying hard to consolidate its strategic interests in West Asia under its 'Look West' policy.

Understanding the CPEC requires an appreciation of China's security concerns, especially those that stem from its ethnic Uighur community in the western region of Xinjiang. Political violence and schemes pushing against economic development are prevalent in that region. Both the Uighur militant groups and the East Turkestan Islamic Movement (ETIM) have sought refuge in the Pakistan-Afghanistan border areas, where they have established links with other terrorist organizations. China perceives the ETIM as a persistent threat committed to targeting their nation. Now, it is important to consider whether China, in the hope of better securing its own territory, will seek to tackle the threat of the jihadi organizations in neighboring Pakistan. In this context, the CPEC represents an international extension of China's effort to deliver security through economic development. Pakistan's military leaders believe that if Chinese investments can turn around the nation's sagging economic fortunes, they will also strengthen the state against foreign challengers like India and the United States, as well as domestic ones like the anti-state insurgent movements. Investments in Pakistan are intended to create jobs, reduce anti-state sentiment, and generate public resources for additional improvements in law and order. Last but not least, the CPEC deal will bring good news for Pakistan, particularly in terms of dealing with some of its major developmental issues like infrastructure and energy shortage.

The Pakistani government has unveiled four highway routes for the project: a western route through Baluchistan and Khyber Pakhtunkhwa province; an eastern route primarily through Sindh and Punjab provinces; a central route crisscrossing the country; and a northern highway route that connects to Kashgar via the Karakoram highway. These routes are a major symbol of China-Pakistan cooperation. Furthermore, a Gwadar to Khunjerab fast-track friendship rail link was also included in the long-term projects to be completed by 2030. Beijing and Islamabad have been close partners for decades. In fact, Pakistan's relations with Beijing are so close that officials call China their "Iron Brother." But the CPEC is a reflection of escalated and enhanced bilateral cooperation at a time of rising Chinese geopolitical ambition and persistent concerns about Pakistan's security and development. Another important question that arises out of the CPEC project is whether Beijing is taking precautionary measures to counter the US-Indian rapprochement?

However, the security dilemma between China and India in the Indian Ocean Region (IOR) is a serious matter of concern. India is highly dependent on energy imports and has progressively sought to secure shipping

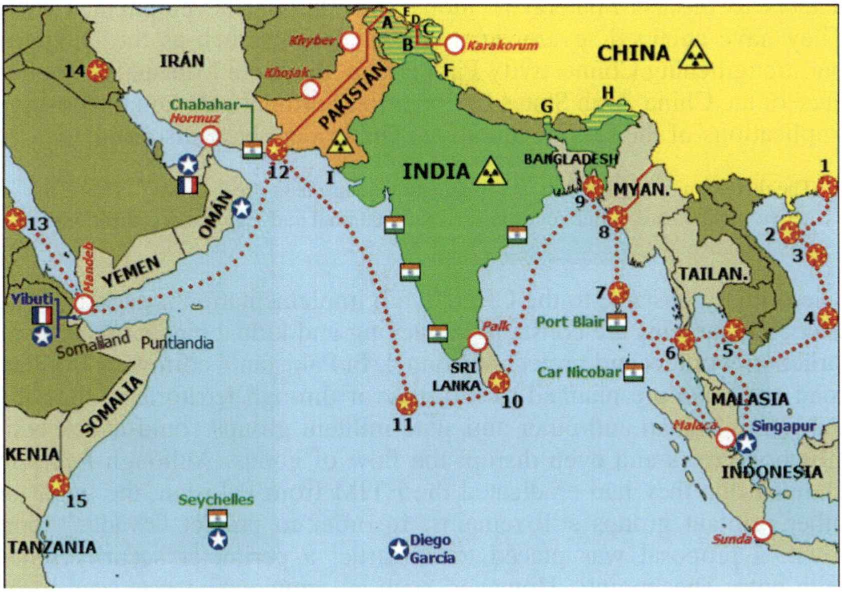

Figure 4 The "String of Pearls" in the Indian Ocean. Source: https://commons.wikimedia.org/wiki/File:Collardeperlaschino.png.

lanes for the transportation of oil from Iran, Myanmar, and Sudan. Any disruptions in the Indian Ocean can lead to serious consequences for the Indian economy. Hence, this region has become strategically significant for India. Nearly half of global seaborne trade passes through the Indian Ocean, around 40 percent of offshore oil production comes from the Indian Ocean, and 65 percent of the world's oil and 35 percent[18] of its gas reserves are found in the littoral states of the IOR. Figure 4 shows how India views the 'string of pearls' in the Indian Ocean Region. The most important 'pearls' are the port of Gwadar (in Pakistan); Hambantota port (in Sri Lanka); Chittagong port (in Bangladesh); the Sittwe port (in Myanmar); and the Maldives.

Conclusion

The OBOR initiative was first proposed by China. Since then, it has become their dream to execute this opportunity on a global scale. Beijing is trying hard to turn it into a common global aspiration by promoting open discussion, policy communication, and coordination among the BRI countries and beyond. President Xi Jinping and Premier Li Keqiang have visited over more than 20 countries and met with their leaders to discuss bilateral relations and regional development issues. They have attended several international forums such as the Dialogue on Strengthening Connectivity Partnership, the Sixth Ministerial Conference of the China-Arab States Cooperation Forum. to explain the positive implications of the OBOR initiative. The leaders have also said:

> The development of the Belt and Road is open and inclusive, and we welcome the active participation of all countries and international and regional organizations in this Initiative.[19]

The primary obstacle to the CPEC's full implementation is security. The Baloch insurgents are constantly attacking and kidnapping Chinese construction workers and project personnel. In Pakistan's northwest frontier, road networks are planned to run near or through territories where the Pakistani Taliban and other anti-state militant groups could attack construction crews and even disrupt the flow of goods. Although Pakistan claimed that they had eradicated the ETIM from Pakistan, the threat of other militant groups still remains. In order to protect Gwadar's port town, a proposal was placed to construct a perimeter security fence with entry checkpoints. However, such an arrangement was seen to be impractical because it would single out local communities, and make it even harder for the implementation of the CPEC deal. Thus, CPEC is swiftly turning into a controversial project. CPEC's viability will remain in doubt and the optimism surrounding it, short-lived, unless Beijing formulates a forward-looking strategy that shows that the China's move is purely commercial in nature and that it is willing to enhance its vision by employing a softer and a more diplomatic tone.

Pakistan has to take care of its own security issues or else the project will fail to deliver commercial success. But, if successful, the CPEC could provide important benefits to Pakistan's economy, which would hopefully lead to future political stability. This project will pull Pakistan into a geostrategic orbit, and also change the face of the region. On the other hand, China's own tolerance for attacks is difficult to comprehend. The CPEC is a flagship of the OBOR initiative, but will China be willing to weather more violence because of that? Beijing might even suffer a political backlash because of fears of domination by Asia's biggest economy. Although the successful implementation of the project will serve as a model for enhancing connectivity and cooperation through similar projects with neighbouring countries, including Afghanistan, Iran, West Asia, and even Europe, there are still many problems to be faced.

To conclude, Silk Road commerce should aim to bring peaceful resolutions to hostile communities, enhance effective diplomatic contracts, and finally, become the symbol for modern international commerce. Beijing's reemergence and reintegration – mainly in the form of Silk Road economic dynamism – will depend on several factors, including how well BRI nations are willing to negotiate with each other. Most of the initiatives associated with the BRI are still in the planning stages. We also need to wait and see how many initiatives will actually be implemented. Only time will tell if China is heading in the right direction and if CPEC will be the road to the future.

NOTES

1. Quotes from leaders at China's New Silk Road meeting, AP, 2017. https://www.foxbusiness.com/markets/quotes-from-leaders-at-chinas-new-silk-road-meeting (accessed 17 January 2019).
2. George Friedman, The World Explained in Maps. Mauldin Economics. https://mauldineconomics.com/download/the-world-explained-in-maps-free-e-book (accessed 16 January 2019).
3. 'Making 'Chinese Dream' a Reality'. ChinaDaily.com.cn, 2013. Retrieved on 30 January 2019. http://www.chinadaily.com.cn/china/2013-12/08/content_17160305.htm

4. 'Belt and Road: China's Grand Gambit', Winter 2016. HSBC. https://www.weekinchina.com/zine/focus-editions/belt-and-road/
5. 'Vision and Actions on Jointly Building Silk Road Economic Belt and 21st-Century Maritime Silk Road'. Issued by the National Development and Reform Commission, Ministry of Foreign Affairs, and Ministry of Commerce of the People's Republic of China, 2015. Retrieved on 18 January 2019. http://en.ndrc.gov.cn/newsrelease/201503/t20150330_669367.html
6. Harry Roberts, 'The Rational Behind the China-Pakistan Economic Corridor: The View from Beijing', in David Lane and Guichang Zhu (Eds.), *Changing Regional Alliances for China and the West*. Lexington Books, 2018.
7. 'The Belt and Road Initiative'. Hong Kong Trade Development Council, May 2018. Retrieved on 2 January 2019. http://china-trade-research.hktdc.com/business-news/article/The-Belt-and-Road-Initiative/The-Belt-and-Road-Initiative-Country-Profiles/obor/en/1/1X000000/1X0A36I0.htm
8. Arif Rafiq, 'The China-Pakistan Economic Corridor: Barriers and Impact'. U.S. Institute of Peace, 25 October 2017.
9. 'Exclusive: CPEC Master Plan Revealed'. Dawn, 15 May 2017. Retrieved on 30 January 2019: https://www.dawn.com/news/1333101
10. Rear Admiral S. Kulshrestha, 'A Tale of Two Ports: Gwadar versus Chabahar'. New Westminster College, Canada. Retrieved from: http://worldnewsreport.in/a-tale-of-two-ports-gwadar-versus-chahbahar/
11. Daniel Markey and James West, 'Behind China's Gambit in Pakistan'. CFR, 2016. https://www.cfr.org/expert-brief/behind-chinas-gambit-pakistan
12. Ian Storey, 'China's 'Malacca Dilemma''. *China Brief* Vol. 6. Issue 8 (12 April 2006).
13. Quotes from leaders at China's New Silk Road meeting, AP, 2017. https://www.foxbusiness.com/markets/quotes-from-leaders-at-chinas-new-silk-road-meeting (accessed 17 January 2019).
14. 'China's Xi Jinping Agrees $46bn Superhighway to Pakistan'. BBC.com, April 2015. https://www.bbc.com/news/world-asia-32377088
15. Ibid.
16. Rear Admiral S. Kulshrestha, 'A Tale of Two Ports: Gwadar versus Chabahar', op. cit.
17. Mohammad Iqbal Chawla, 'One Belt One Road Summit 2017 and its Implications for CPEC: An Overview'. *Research Journal of South Asian Studies* Vol. 32. Issue 2 (2017): 277–284.
18. K. Acharya Arabinda, 'India and Southeast Asia in the Age of Terror: Building Partnerships for Peace'. *Contemporary Southeast Asia* Vol. 28. Issue 2 (2006): 297–321.
19. 'Vision and Actions on Jointly Building Silk Road Economic Belt and 21st-Century Maritime Silk Road', op. cit.

Notes for Contributors

Submissions: The Editor welcomes submission of material for consideration as a main article or a review article. Comments on articles previously published in *Asian Affairs* can also be submitted ideally in the form of a letter to the Editor. Main articles should be broadly consistent with the 'Aims and Scope' of *Asian Affairs* (see inside front cover), and generally be approximately 5000–7000 words in length. They should include a bibliographical note on the author of no more than 50 words. Contributors **must** also submit a one-paragraph summary or abstract of their article when making any submission. Review articles should be in the range of 1500–2000 words and cover several books. Book reviews should be 650–700 words for single titles or 1000 words for two titles, although shorter reviews are welcomed. Submissions should be made by email in an attached Microsoft Word file. Email address is: editor@rsaa.org.uk or bijan.omrani@btinternet.com. Email messages concerning book reviews may also be addressed to Richard Fell at richardfell@btinternet.com. Potential contributors are strongly urged to look at past issues of *Asian Affairs* or its articles published online to acquaint themselves with the house style.

Presentation: Manuscripts should be typed in journal style (Times New Roman, 12 pt font), on one side only. Please paginate the whole text. Authors should provide their postal and email addresses, telephone number and/or fax number.

Endnotes and references: Endnotes and references should be indicated in the text by superscript 1, 2, 3, etc. at the end of the relevant sentence and listed at the end of the paper in numerical order. Endnotes should be inserted using the 'insert endnote' function in Microsoft Word. Articles whose endnotes have not been entered in this manner will be returned to the contributor for initial reformatting. Endnotes should elaborate on points made in the text, indicate sources of relevant research or refer to sources for further information. The use of endnotes should be kept to a minimum. They should be used only in the case of little-known or contentious facts. Multiple citations for a point of fact should not be included; single citations of a reliable source are regarded as sufficient. References should be written in the following style:

R. Shadlen, 'Southeast Asia – Before and After'. *Foreign Affairs* Vol. 53. Issue 3 (1975): 553.

T. Clark and M. Derhalli, *Al-Mansur's Book On Hunting*. Warminster: Aris & Phillips, 2001.

B. Kiernan, 'The Samlaut Rebellion, 1967–68', in B. Kiernan & C. Boua (Eds.), *Peasants and Politics in Kampuchea, 1942–1981*. London: Zed Press, 1982, pp. 166–167.

Book Reviews: Book titles should conform to the following pattern:

Author, or Author & Author (first name surname) (ed) or (eds). *Title.* Series. Publisher, place of publication, date of publication, pages, (Roman numerals + Arabic numerals). Maps. Illust. etc. Hardback or paperback. Price. ISBN (paperback price and ISBN, if in addition).

For example:

Mark Bassin. *Imperial Visions: Nationalist Imagination and Geographical Expansion in the Russian Far East, 1840–1865.* Cambridge Studies in Historical Geography, Cambridge University Press. Cambridge, 1999. pp. 329. Maps. Notes. Bibliog. Index. Hb. £47.50. ISBN 0 5213 9174 1

Usha Haley & Frank-Jürgen Richter (eds). *Asian Post-Crisis Management: Corporate and Governmental Strategies for Sustainable Competitive Advantage.* Palgrave/Macmillan, London, 2002. pp. 451. Tables. Figs. Notes. Refs. Index. Hb. £50. ISBN 0 3339 4964 1

Illustrations: Maps and figures should be clear and large enough to be suitable for reproduction and the lettering should be large enough to allow (if necessary) reduction in size for printing. All maps, diagrams and other drawings should be referred to as figures, and should be numbered consecutively in Arabic numerals in the order in which they are referred to in the text. Captions to figures, giving the appropriate figure number, should be typed on a separate page at the end of the article. Photographs (as prints rather than slides) should be submitted with captions and their position in the text should be marked as Plate 1, 2, 3, etc. in brackets. Permission to reproduce copyright material must be obtained by the author prior to submission and any acknowledgements should be included either in the text or the caption as appropriate.

Free article access: As an author, you will receive free access to your article on Taylor & Francis Online. You will be given access to the *My authored works* section of Taylor & Francis Online, which shows you all your published articles. You can easily view, read, and download your published articles from there. In addition, if someone has cited your article, you will be able to see this information. We are committed to promoting and increasing the visibility of your article and have provided http://journalauthors.tandf.co.uk/beyondpublication/promotearticle.asp.

Reprints and journal copies: Corresponding authors can receive 50 free reprints of their article or book review. For enquiries regarding reprints, please contact the Taylor & Francis Author Services team at reprints@tandf.co.uk. Corresponding authors of full articles will receive a complimentary copy of the issue containing their article. To order extra copies of the issue containing your article, please contact our Customer Services team at Adhoc@tandf.co.uk.

Copyright: It is a condition of publication that all contributing authors grant to The Royal Society for Asian Affairs the necessary rights to the copyright in all articles submitted to the Journal, which is published for The Royal Society for Asian Affairs by Taylor & Francis. Authors are required sign an Article Publishing Agreement to facilitate this. This will ensure the widest dissemination and protection against copyright infringement of articles. The "article" is defined as comprising the final, definitive, and citable Version of Scholarly Record, and includes: (*a*) the accepted manuscript in its final and revised form, including the text, abstract, and all accompanying tables, illustrations, data; and (*b*) any supplementary material. Copyright policy is explained in detail at http://journalauthors.tandf.co.uk/preparation/copyright.asp.

Index

For Product Safety Concerns and Information please contact our EU representative GPSR@taylorandfrancis.com Taylor & Francis Verlag GmbH, Kaufingerstraße 24, 80331 München, Germany

Batch number: 10726532

Printed by Printforce, the Netherlands